Grammar +Plus Writing

START

3

DARAKWON

저자 약력

전지원

미국 오리건 주립대 Linguistics 석사
(현) 한국 외국어대학교 외국어연수 평가원 영어 전임강사
〈내공 중학 영작문〉 (다락원), 〈Grammar Mate〉 (다락원),
〈Grammar's Cool〉 (YBM), 〈빠르게 잡는 영문법〉 (천재교육) 등 다수의 교재 공저

박혜영

미국 하와이 주립대 Second Language Studies 석사
(현) 한국 외국어대학교 외국어연수 평가원 영어 전임강사
〈내공 중학 영작문〉 (다락원), 〈Grammar Mate〉 (다락원),
〈Grammar's Cool〉 (YBM), 〈빠르게 잡는 영문법〉 (천재교육) 등 다수의 교재 공저

Grammar +lus Writing START ❸

지은이 전지원, 박혜영
펴낸이 정규도
펴낸곳 (주)다락원

개정판 1쇄 발행 2023년 12월 11일
개정판 2쇄 발행 2024년 2월 26일

편집 홍인표, 안혜원, 서정아
디자인 김민지, 포레스트
영문 감수 Michael A. Putlack

📚**다락원** 경기도 파주시 문발로 211
내용문의 (02) 736-2031 내선 500
구입문의 (02) 736-2031 내선 250~252
Fax (02) 732-2037
출판등록 1977년 9월 16일 제406-2008-000007호

ISBN 978-89-277-8070-0 64740
      978-89-277-8067-0 64740(set)

http://www.darakwon.co.kr

다락원 홈페이지를 방문하시면 상세한 출판 정보와 함께 동영상 강좌,
MP3 자료 등의 다양한 어학 정보를 얻으실 수 있습니다.

Grammar +Plus Writing

START

3

STRUCTURES 구성과 특징

Grammar Plus Writing START 시리즈는

- 각 문법 사항을 이해하기 쉽게 구성하여 기초 영문법을 쉽고 재미있게 학습할 수 있습니다.
- 학습한 문법 요소를 영작과 연계하여 문법 지식과 영작 능력을 동시에 향상시킬 수 있습니다.
- 학교 내신 및 서술형 문제에 효과적으로 대비할 수 있습니다.

문법 설명

사진과 함께 대표 예문을 확인하고, 표를 통해 핵심 문법 사항을 간략히 정리할 수 있어요.

PRACTICE

문제를 통해 학습한 내용을 이해했는지 바로 체크해볼 수 있어요.

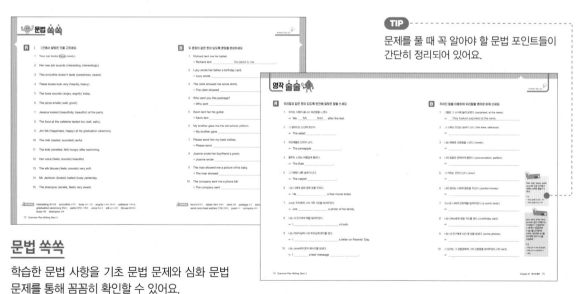

TIP

문제를 풀 때 꼭 알아야 할 문법 포인트들이 간단히 정리되어 있어요.

문법 쏙쏙

학습한 문법 사항을 기초 문법 문제와 심화 문법 문제를 통해 꼼꼼히 확인할 수 있어요.

영작 술술

학습한 문법 사항을 영작과 연계하여 연습할 수 있어요. 영작 술술 A는 본격적인 영작에 들어가기 전 준비 과정으로 활용할 수 있으며, B에서는 완전한 영어 문장을 써 볼 수 있어요.

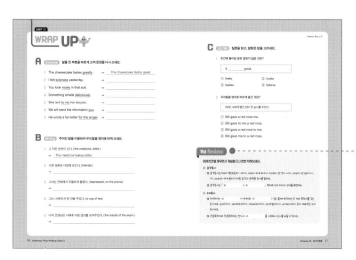

WRAP UP

각 Unit에서 배운 내용을 문법·영작·내신 문제를
통해 다시 한번 정리할 수 있어요.

개념 REVIEW

꼭 기억해야 할 중요 문법 개념들을 빈칸 채우기를
통해 복습할 수 있어요.

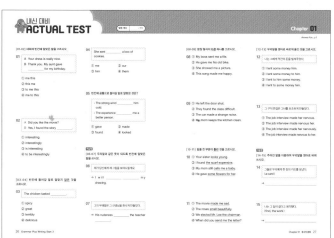

내신 대비 ACTUAL TEST

챕터가 끝날 때마다 배운 내용을 종합적으로 확인
해 볼 수 있어요. 다양한 내신 유형과 서술형 문제에
대비할 수 있으며, 자신의 실력을 평가할 수 있어요.

WORKBOOK

1 Grammar & Writing Practice

본책에서 학습한 내용을 A에서는 문법 문제,
B에서는 영작 문제를 통해 복습할 수 있어요.

2 Word Practice

본문에서 쓰인 필수 어휘를 듣고 따라 쓰며, 영작
에 유용한 단어들을 복습하고 정리할 수 있어요.

온라인 부가자료 | www.darakwon.co.kr
다락원 홈페이지에서 무료로 부가자료를 다운로드
하거나 웹에서 이용할 수 있습니다.

CONTENTS 목차

01

동사의 종류

학습목표

1 감각동사와 수여동사의 의미와 쓰임에 대해 알아봐요.

2 목적보어를 갖는 동사에 대해 알아보고, 형용사를 목적보어로 취하는 동사와 명사를 목적보어로 취하는 동사를 구분해요.

UNIT 01 감각동사 / 수여동사

1 감각동사

The cupcakes **look** delicious.

The roses **smell** nice.

감각동사	감각동사 + 형용사	
feel, look, taste, smell, sound 등	I **feel** *good*.	나는 기분이 좋다.
	You **look** *happy*.	너는 행복해 보인다.
	This soup **tastes** *salty*.	이 수프는 짠맛이 난다.
	The flowers **smell** *sweet*.	그 꽃들은 향긋한 냄새가 난다.
	This song **sounds** *beautiful*.	이 노래는 아름답게 들린다.

☑ **감각동사**는 **feel**(기분 ~하다), **look**(~하게 보이다), **taste**(~한 맛이 나다), **smell**(~한 냄새가 나다), **sound**(~하게 들리다)처럼 감각과 관련된 동사를 말해요.

☑ 감각동사는 「**감각동사 + 형용사**」 형태로 쓰여 주어의 상태를 표현해요.
e.g. You **look** *happily*. (X)

PRACTICE 1 알맞은 말 고르기

❶ Honey ((tastes), sounds) sweet.

❷ The music (smells, sounds) great.

❸ These shoes (feel, taste) a bit tight.

❹ That shirt (looks, smells) good on you.

2 수여동사

Lisa **gave** her mom a gift.

Rachel **lent** me a book.

수여동사	수여동사 + 간접목적어 + 직접목적어	
give, send, show, lend, write 등	Tom **gave** her *his pen*.	Tom은 그녀에게 그의 펜을 주었다.
	I **sent** my sister *a postcard*.	나는 나의 언니에게 엽서를 보냈다.
	Erin **showed** us *a picture*.	Erin은 우리에게 사진을 보여주었다.
	My brother **lent** me *five dollars*.	나의 형은 나에게 5달러를 빌려주었다.
	He **wrote** Jane *an email*.	그는 Jane에게 이메일을 썼다.

☑ **수여동사**는 **간접목적어**(~에게)와 **직접목적어**(~을 / 를)에 해당하는 두 개의 목적어를 갖는 동사예요. give(주다), send(보내주다), show(보여주다), lend(빌려주다), write(써주다) 등이 대표적인 수여동사예요.

☑ 간접목적어와 직접목적어는 전치사 **to**를 사용해서 순서를 바꿀 수 있어요.
  e.g. Tom **gave** her *his pen*. → Tom **gave** *his pen* **to** her.

PRACTICE 2 문장 전환하기

❶ He gave her a doll. ➡ He gave a doll ___to___ ___her___.

❷ I lent him my umbrella. ➡ I lent my umbrella _____ _____.

❸ I wrote Bill a letter. ➡ I wrote a letter _____ _____.

❹ She showed us a map. ➡ She showed a map _____ _____.

A ( ) 안에서 알맞은 것을 고르세요.

1 Your car looks (new, newly).

2 Her new job sounds (interesting, interestingly).

3 This smoothie doesn't taste (sweetness, sweet).

4 These boxes look very (heavily, heavy).

5 The boss sounds (angry, angrily) today.

6 The pizza smells (well, good).

7 Jessica looked (beautifully, beautiful) at the party.

8 The food at the cafeteria tasted too (salt, salty).

9 Jim felt (happiness, happy) at his graduation ceremony.

10 The milk (tasted, sounded) awful.

11 The kids (smelled, felt) hungry after swimming.

12 Her voice (feels, sounds) beautiful.

13 The silk blouse (feels, sounds) very soft.

14 Mr. Jackson (looked, tasted) busy yesterday.

15 The shampoo (smells, feels) very sweet.

 WORDS   interesting 흥미로운   smoothie 스무디   boss 상사, 사장   angrily 노하여, 화내어   cafeteria 구내식당
graduation ceremony 졸업식   awful 끔찍한, 지독한   voice 목소리   silk 실크, 비단   blouse 블라우스
busy 바쁜   shampoo 샴푸

B 두 문장이 같은 뜻이 되도록 문장을 완성하세요.

1 Richard lent me his tablet.

= Richard lent _____ his tablet to me _____ .

2 Lucy wrote her father a birthday card.

= Lucy wrote _____ .

3 The clerk showed me some shirts.

= The clerk showed _____ .

4 Who sent you this package?

= Who sent _____ ?

5 Kevin lent her his guitar.

= Kevin lent _____ .

6 My brother gave me his old school uniform.

= My brother gave _____ .

7 Please send him my best wishes.

= Please send _____ .

8 Joanne wrote her boyfriend a poem.

= Joanne wrote _____ .

9 The man showed me a picture of his baby.

= The man showed _____ .

10 The company sent me a phone bill.

= The company sent _____ .

WORDS lend 빌려주다　tablet 태블릿 컴퓨터　clerk 점원　package 소포　school uniform 교복
send one's best wishes 안부를 전하다　poem 시　company 회사　bill 고지서, 청구서

A 우리말과 같은 뜻이 되도록 빈칸에 알맞은 말을 쓰세요.

1 우리는 시험이 끝나고 피곤함을 느꼈다.

➡ We ___felt___ ___tired___ after the test.

2 그 샐러드는 신선해 보인다.

➡ The salad _____ _____.

3 파인애플은 단맛이 난다.

➡ The pineapple _____ _____.

4 플루트 소리는 아름답게 들린다.

➡ The flute _____ _____.

5 그 카펫은 나쁜 냄새가 난다.

➡ The carpet _____ _____.

6 그는 나에게 공짜 영화 표를 주었다.

➡ He _____ _____ a free movie ticket.

7 Joe는 우리에게 그의 가족 사진을 보여주었다.

➡ Joe _____ _____ a photo of his family.

8 나는 내 친구에게 책을 빌려주었다.

➡ I _____ _____ _____ a book.

9 나는 어버이날에 나의 부모님께 편지를 썼다.

➡ I _____ _____ _____ a letter on Parents' Day.

10 나는 Jane에게 문자 메시지를 보냈다.

➡ I _____ a text message _____ _____.

B 주어진 말을 이용하여 우리말을 영어로 바꿔 쓰세요.

1 그들은 그 소식에 놀라 보였다. (surprised, at the news)

➡   They looked surprised at the news.

2 그 스튜는 맛있는 냄새가 난다. (the stew, delicious)

➡ _____

3 나는 때때로 외로움을 느낀다. (lonely)

➡ _____

4 너의 발음은 완벽하게 들린다. (pronunciation, perfect)

➡ _____

5 그 커피는 신맛이 난다. (sour)

➡ _____

6 나의 엄마는 나에게 용돈을 주신다. (pocket money)

➡ _____

7 Tom은 나에게 만화책을 빌려주었다. (a comic book)

➡ _____

8 나는 Mike에게 생일 카드를 썼다. (a birthday card)

➡ _____

9 나는 내 친구에게 사진 몇 장을 보냈다. (some photos)

➡ _____

10 그 남자는 그 경찰관에게 그의 신분증을 보여주었다. (ID card)

➡ _____

TIP 1

feel, look, taste, smell, sound와 같은 감각동사 뒤에는 보어로 형용사가 와요.

e.g.
- You look sadly. (x)
- You look sad. (o)

TIP 2

give, send, show, lend, write와 같은 수여동사는 「수여동사 + 간접목적어 (~에게) + 직접목적어 (~을/를)」의 형태로 쓰여요. 목적어의 순서를 바꾸려면 전치사 to를 사용해요.

e.g.
- He gave me a book.
- He gave a book to me.

WRAP UP

A　Grammar　밑줄 친 부분을 바르게 고쳐 문장을 다시 쓰세요.

1　The cheesecake tastes greatly.　➡　The cheesecake tastes great.

2　I felt sickness yesterday.　➡　_____

3　You look nicely in that suit.　➡　_____

4　Something smells deliciously.　➡　_____

5　She lent to me her bicycle.　➡　_____

6　We will send the information you.　➡　_____

7　He wrote a fan letter for the singer.　➡　_____

B　Writing　주어진 말을 이용하여 우리말을 영어로 바꿔 쓰세요.

1　그 약은 쓴맛이 난다. (the medicine, bitter)

➡　The medicine tastes bitter.

2　너희 삼촌은 다정해 보인다. (friendly)

➡　_____

3　그녀는 전화에서 우울하게 들렸다. (depressed, on the phone)

➡　_____

4　그는 나에게 차 한 잔을 주었다. (a cup of tea)

➡　_____

5　나의 선생님은 나에게 시험 결과를 보여주었다. (the results of the exam)

➡　_____

C 내신 대비 질문을 읽고, 알맞은 답을 고르세요.

1 빈칸에 들어갈 말로 알맞지 <u>않은</u> 것은?

> It _____ good.

① feels   ② looks

③ tastes   ④ listens

2 우리말을 영어로 바르게 옮긴 것은?

> Bill은 나에게 빨간 장미 한 송이를 주었다.

① Bill gave a red rose me.

② Bill gave to me a red rose.

③ Bill gave a red rose to me.

④ Bill gave me to a red rose.

개념 Review

아래 빈칸을 채우면서 개념을 다시 한번 익혀보세요.

❶ **감각동사**

☑ 감각동사는 feel(기분[촉감]이 ~하다), look(~하게 보이다), taste(~한 맛이 나다), smell(~한 냄새가 나다), sound(~하게 들리다)처럼 감각과 관련된 동사를 말해요.

☑ 감각동사는 「❶ _____ + ❷ _____」 형태로 쓰여 주어의 상태를 표현해요.

❷ **수여동사**

☑ 수여동사는 ❸ _____ (~에게)와 ❹ _____ (~을 / 를)에 해당하는 두 개의 목적어를 갖는 동사예요. give(주다), send(보내주다), show(보여주다), lend(빌려주다), write(써주다) 등이 대표적인 수여동사예요.

☑ 간접목적어와 직접목적어는 전치사 ❺ _____ 를 사용해서 순서를 바꿀 수 있어요.

UNIT 02 목적보어를 갖는 동사

1 동사+목적어+형용사

This movie **makes** me sad.

Jenny **keeps** her house clean.

형용사 목적보어를 갖는 동사

make, keep, leave, find 등	My dog **makes** me *happy*. This coat **keeps** you *warm*. He **left** the door *open*. I **found** the book *interesting*.	나의 개는 나를 행복하게 만든다. 이 코트는 너를 따뜻하게 해준다. 그는 그 문을 열어두었다. 나는 그 책이 흥미롭다고 생각했다.

☑ **목적보어**는 목적어 뒤에 위치하여 목적어의 성질이나 상태를 보충 설명해주는 말이에요.

☑ 동사 **make**(만들다), **keep**(유지하다), **leave**(두다), **find**(생각하다, 알아채다)는 목적보어로 **형용사**가 와요.
   e.g. My dog **makes** me *happy*. (me = happy)

PRACTICE 1 알맞은 형용사 고르기

awake	boring	fat	open

❶ Fast food makes you ____fat____.

❷ I found the movie a little _____.

❸ Please leave the window _____.

❹ The mosquitoes kept me _____ all night.

2 동사＋목적어＋명사

I **named** my cat Angel.

We **elected** Kate our team captain.

명사 목적보어를 갖는 동사		
call, name, make, elect 등	My parents **call** me *Princess*.	나의 부모님은 나를 공주라고 부른다.
	I **named** my dog *Pluto*.	나는 나의 개를 플루토라고 이름 지었다.
	The movie **made** her *a star*.	그 영화는 그녀를 스타로 만들었다.
	They **elected** him *president*.	그들은 그를 대통령으로 선출했다.

☑ 동사 **call**(부르다), **name**(이름 짓다), **make**(만들다), **elect**(선출하다)는 목적보어로 **명사**가 와요.

I **named** my dog *Pluto*. (my dog = Pluto)

☑ 위의 동사들은 수여동사와 비슷한 문장 형태를 이루지만 다르게 해석되므로 구별해서 알아두어야 해요.

e.g. I gave him *a book*. (him ≠ a book)

PRACTICE **2** 알맞은 동사 넣기

call   elected   made   named

❶ My name is Jonathan, but people ____call____ me John.

❷ We _____ Eric class president.

❸ They _____ their baby daughter Jennifer.

❹ The book _____ him a famous writer.

문법 쏙쏙

A 주어진 말을 바르게 배열하여 문장을 완성하세요.

1 makes / this song / happy / me / .

→   This song makes me happy.

2 helpful / the book / I / found / .

→ _____

3 awake / coffee / me / keeps / .

→ _____

4 sad / made / the news / people / .

→ _____

5 keep / healthy / you / fresh vegetables / .

→ _____

6 found / very kind / the clerk / I / .

→ _____

7 fun / the clown / the party / made / .

→ _____

8 left / the house / messy / they / .

→ _____

9 his part-time job / him / busy / keeps / .

→ _____

10 found / they / the situation / serious / .

→ _____

WORDS   helpful 도움이 되는   awake 깨어 있는   clown 광대   messy 지저분한
part-time job 시간제 근무, 아르바이트   situation 상황   serious 심각한

B 주어진 말을 바르게 배열하여 문장을 완성하세요.

1 the boy / the goldfish / named / Nemo / .

→ The boy named the goldfish Nemo.

2 made / a famous actor / him / the movie / .

→ _____

3 elected / we / class president / Minho / .

→ _____

4 named / they / the Golden Gate / the bridge / .

→ _____

5 call / a kitty / a cat / some people / .

→ _____

6 the man / made / the invention / a millionaire / .

→ _____

7 her hamster / she / Charley / named / .

→ _____

8 him / the 15th president / elected / they / .

→ _____

9 me / a better person / books / make / .

→ _____

10 Mr. Kim / we / the chairman / elected / .

→ _____

 WORDS goldfish 금붕어 **name** 이름 짓다; 이름 **actor** 배우 **elect** 선출하다 **president** 회장, 대통령
bridge 다리 **kitty** 고양이, (애칭) 야옹이 **invention** 발명(품) **millionaire** 백만장자 **hamster** 햄스터
better 더 나은 **chairman** 의장, 회장

영작 술술

A 우리말과 같은 뜻이 되도록 빈칸에 알맞은 말을 쓰세요.

1 그 오랜 비행은 나를 피곤하게 만들었다.

➡ The long flight ___made___ me ___tired___.

2 우리는 그 낱말 맞추기 게임이 어렵다고 생각했다.

➡ We _____ the crossword puzzle _____.

3 그 소음은 밤새도록 나를 깨어 있게 했다.

➡ The noise _____ me _____ all night.

4 그는 차의 창문을 열어두었다.

➡ He _____ the car window _____.

5 사람들은 그 곰을 Pooh라고 부른다.

➡ People _____ the bear _____.

6 Lucy는 그녀의 개를 Jack이라고 이름 지었다.

➡ Lucy _____ her dog _____.

7 우리는 Mike를 우리 독서회의 지도자로 선출했다.

➡ We _____ _____ the leader of our book club.

8 나는 그의 행동이 이상하다고 생각했다.

➡ I _____ his behavior _____.

9 이 노래는 그를 스타로 만들었다.

➡ This song _____ _____ a star.

10 저를 혼자 내버려 두세요.

➡ Please _____ me _____.

B 주어진 말을 이용하여 우리말을 영어로 바꿔 쓰세요.

1 비는 나를 우울하게 만든다. (make, depressed)

➡ Rain makes me depressed.

2 그 일은 나를 온종일 바쁘게 했다. (keep, all day)

➡

3 나는 과학 수업이 어렵다고 생각했다. (find, the science class)

➡

4 그는 그 문을 잠그지 않은 채로 두었다. (leave, unlocked)

➡

5 벽난로는 우리를 따뜻하게 해준다. (the fireplace, keep)

➡

6 나는 나의 부모님을 엄마와 아빠라고 부른다. (Mom and Dad)

➡

7 그들은 그들의 아들을 David라고 이름 지었다. (their son)

➡

8 우리 클럽은 Ryan을 회장으로 선출했다. (president)

➡

9 그 복권은 그를 백만장자로 만들었다. (the lottery, a millionaire)

➡

10 그녀는 그녀의 부모님을 자랑스럽게 만들었다. (proud)

➡

TIP 1

make, keep, leave, find와 같은 동사는 목적보어로 형용사가 와요.

e.g.
- He made me angry.
  (me = angry)
- I found the game exciting.
  (the game = exciting)

TIP 2

call, name, make, elect와 같은 동사는 목적보어로 명사가 와요.

e.g.
- They called him a liar.
  (him = a liar)
- He named his dog Spot.
  (his dog = Spot)

WRAP UP

A Grammar [보기]에서 알맞은 말을 골라 문장을 완성하세요.

| a teen idol   easy   clean   delicious   happy   Violet |

1 His daughter makes him _____happy_____.

2 She always keeps her room _____.

3 They found the exam _____.

4 Jane named her cat _____.

5 The song made him _____.

6 I found the meal _____.

B Writing 주어진 말을 이용하여 우리말을 영어로 바꿔 쓰세요.

1 그는 그의 아내를 "honey"라고 부른다. (wife)

➡ He calls his wife "honey."

2 나는 그 그림이 아름답다고 생각했다. (find, the painting)

➡ _____

3 그들은 그를 의장으로 선출했다. (the chairman)

➡ _____

4 그 소설은 그 작가를 유명하게 만들었다. (the novel, the writer)

➡ _____

5 이 양말은 당신의 발을 따뜻하게 해준다. (these socks, keep)

➡ _____

C [내신 대비] 질문을 읽고, 알맞은 답을 고르세요.

1 밑줄 친 부분이 틀린 것은?

① I found him <u>funny</u>.

② She left the door <u>open</u>.

③ The ice keeps the water <u>cool</u>.

④ Small gifts make people <u>happily</u>.

2 우리말을 영어로 바르게 옮긴 것은?

> 그 어미 오리들은 그들의 알을 따뜻하게 품었다.

① The mother ducks kept warm their eggs.

② The mother ducks kept their eggs warm.

③ The mother ducks kept their eggs warmly.

④ The mother ducks kept warm to their eggs.

개념 Review

아래 빈칸을 채우면서 개념을 다시 한번 익혀보세요.

❶ 동사 + 목적어 + 형용사

☑ **❶** _____ 는 목적어 뒤에 위치하여 목적어의 성질이나 상태를 보충 설명해주는 말이에요.

☑ 동사 make(만들다), keep(유지하다), leave(두다), find(생각하다, 알아채다)는 목적보어로

❷ _____ 가 와요.

❷ 동사 + 목적어 + 명사

☑ 동사 call(부르다), name(이름 짓다), make(만들다), elect(선출하다)는 목적보어로 **❸** _____

가 와요.

☑ 위의 동사들은 수여동사와 비슷한 문장 형태를 이루지만 다르게 해석되므로 구별해서 알아두어야 해요.

[01-02] 대화의 빈칸에 알맞은 말을 고르시오.

01

> A Your dress is really nice.
> B Thank you. My aunt gave
>   _____ for my birthday.

① me this

② this me

③ to me this

④ me to this

02

> A Did you like the movie?
> B Yes, I found the story _____.

① interesting

② interestingly

③ is interesting

④ to be interestingly

[03-04] 빈칸에 들어갈 말로 알맞지 <u>않은</u> 것을 고르시오.

03

> The chicken tasted _____.

① spicy

② great

③ terribly

④ delicious

04

> She sent _____ a box of cookies.

① me

② our

③ him

④ them

05 빈칸에 공통으로 들어갈 말로 알맞은 것은?

> • The strong wind _____ him cold.
> • The experience _____ me a better person.

① gave

② made

③ found

④ looked

서술형

[06-07] 우리말과 같은 뜻이 되도록 빈칸에 알맞은 말을 쓰시오.

06

> 제가 당신에게 제 그림을 보여드릴게요.

→ I will _____ _____ my drawing.

07

> 그의 무례함은 그 선생님을 화나게 만들었다.

→ His rudeness _____ the teacher _____.

[08-09] 문장 형식이 <u>다른</u> 하나를 고르시오.

08 ① My boss sent me a file.
② He gave me his old bike.
③ She showed me a picture.
④ This song made me happy.

09 ① He left the door shut.
② They found the class difficult.
③ The car made a strange noise.
④ My mom keeps the kitchen clean.

[10-11] 밑줄 친 부분이 틀린 것을 고르시오.

10 ① Your sister <u>looks young</u>.
② I found <u>the scarf expensive</u>.
③ My mom still <u>calls me a baby</u>.
④ He gave <u>some flowers for her</u>.

11 ① The movie <u>made me sad</u>.
② The roses <u>smell beautifully</u>.
③ We <u>elected Mr. Lee the chairman</u>.
④ When did you <u>send me the letter</u>?

[12-13] 우리말을 영어로 바르게 옮긴 것을 고르시오.

12
나는 그에게 약간의 돈을 빌려주었다.

① I lent some money him.
② I lent some money to him.
③ I lent to him some money.
④ I lent to some money him.

13
그 구직 면접은 그녀를 초조하게 만들었다.

① The job interview made her nervous.
② The job interview made nervous her.
③ The job interview made her nervously.
④ The job interview made nervous to her.

서술형

[14-15] 주어진 말을 이용하여 우리말을 영어로 바꿔 쓰시오.

14
그들은 우리에게 한 장의 카드를 보냈다.
(a card)

➡ _____

15
나는 그 일이 쉽다고 생각했다.
(find, the work)

➡ _____

02

조동사

학습목표

1 Can의 의미와 부정문, 의문문을 만드는 방법을 익히고, May의 의미를 알아봐요.

2 Must의 두 가지 의미를 알아보고, Have to의 의미와 부정문, 의문문을 만드는 방법을 익혀요.

UNIT 01 Can / May

1 Can

Fish **can** swim, but they **can't** walk.

Can you ride a skateboard?

문장의 종류		
긍정문	She **can** play the piano. You **can** get there by bus.	그녀는 피아노를 칠 수 있다. 너는 그곳에 버스로 갈 수 있다.
부정문	Penguins **cannot** fly. We **can't** win the game.	펭귄은 날 수 없다. 우리는 경기를 이길 수 없다.
의문문	**Can** you jump high?	너는 높이 뛸 수 있니?

☑ 조동사 can은 '~할 수 있다'라는 의미로 **능력**이나 **가능**을 나타내요. 이때 can과 같은 조동사 뒤에는 반드시 **동사원형**이 와요.
e.g. She can *plays* the piano. (X)

☑ can의 부정문은 **cannot** 또는 **can't**를 사용하고, 의문문은 can을 주어 앞으로 보내서 만들 수 있어요.

PRACTICE 1 문장 완성하기

❶ 그녀는 말을 탈 수 있다. → She _____can_____ _____ride_____ a horse.

❷ 나는 그 파일을 열 수 없다. → I _____ _____ the file.

❸ 너는 한국어를 할 수 있니? → _____ you _____ Korean?

❹ 그는 우리와 같이 갈 수 없다. → He _____ _____ with us.

2 May

She **may** be sick.
She **may not** go to school tomorrow.

May I open this gift box?

의미		
약한 추측 (~일지도 모른다)	She **may** come to the party. He **may not** be at home.	그녀는 파티에 올지도 모른다. 그는 집에 없을지도 모른다.
허락 (~해도 좋다)	You **may** leave early today. **May** I have some tea, please?	오늘은 일찍 가도 좋습니다. 차를 좀 주시겠어요?

☑ 조동사 **may**는 '~일지도 모른다'라는 **약한 추측**의 의미를 나타내고 부정문은 **may not**을 사용해요.

☑ may는 '~해도 좋다'라는 **허락**의 의미를 나타내기도 해요. '~해도 좋습니까?'라고 상대방에게 허락을 구할 때는 'May I ~?'로 물을 수 있어요.

PRACTICE 2 문장 완성하기

❶ 우리는 오늘 밤에 나갈지도 모른다. → We ___may___ ___go___ out tonight.

❷ 그는 그것을 좋아하지 않을지도 모른다. → He _____ _____ _____ it.

❸ 이 방을 써도 좋습니다. → You _____ _____ this room.

❹ 질문을 하나 해도 될까요? → _____ I _____ a question?

A ( ) 안에서 알맞은 것을 고르세요.

1 Jack is a good swimmer. He (can, can't) swim well.

2 I lost my key. I (can, can't) open the door.

3 What sports (can, can't) you play?

4 Sam is hungry. He (can, can't) eat another sandwich.

5 Squirrels (can, can't) climb trees very well.

6 I'm sorry. I (can, can't) help you right now.

7 Jane is very clever. She (can, can't) speak three languages.

8 The baby (can, can't) crawl, but he (can, can't) walk yet.

9 I know Tom very well. I (can, can't) recognize him.

10 His handwriting is very bad. I (can, can't) read it.

11 (Can, Can't) you play any musical instruments?

12 The theater isn't far. You (can, can't) go there on foot.

13 The music is too loud. I (can, can't) hear you.

14 It's really dark. I (can, can't) see anything.

15 Where are my slippers? I (can, can't) find them.

 WORDS another 또 하나(의)   squirrel 다람쥐   clever 영리한   language 언어   crawl (엎드려) 기다   yet 아직
recognize 알아보다   handwriting 필체   musical instrument 악기   theater 극장   on foot 걸어서,
도보로   anything 아무것(도)   slipper 슬리퍼, 실내화

B 주어진 동사와 may를 이용하여 문장을 완성하세요.

1 Susan is absent today. She _____ may be _____ sick. (be)

2 Ben has the flu. He _____ to the party. (come)

3 _____ I _____ a glass of water, please? (have)

4 Try calling Emma. She _____ home by now. (be)

5 You _____ my computer. I'm not using it. (use)

6 He _____ the answer. Let's ask someone else then. (know)

7 Take an umbrella. It _____ later today. (rain)

8 _____ I _____ your driver's license, please? (see)

9 Don't press the button. It _____ dangerous. (be)

10 Where is my pen? – It _____ in your bag. (be)

11 You _____ early today if you want. (leave)

12 He likes music. He _____ to the concert tonight. (go)

13 _____ I _____ in? – Sure. Come on in and take a seat. (come)

14 He _____ his car and buy a new one. (sell)

15 Visitors _____ the campus between 9:00 a.m. and 7:00 p.m. (enter)

WORDS　absent 결석한　flu 독감　by now 지금쯤은　later today 오늘 늦게　driver's license 운전 면허(증)
press 누르다　button 버튼, 단추　take a seat 자리에 앉다　enter 들어가다　campus 캠퍼스, 교내
between 사이에

영작 술술

A 우리말과 같은 뜻이 되도록 빈칸에 알맞은 말을 쓰세요.

1 나는 바이올린을 연주할 수 있다.

➡ I ____can____ ____play____ the violin.

2 너는 종이비행기를 만들 수 있니?

➡ _____ you _____ a paper airplane?

3 나의 할아버지는 잘 들을 수 없다.

➡ My grandfather _____ _____ well.

4 나의 아빠는 트럭을 운전할 수 있다.

➡ My dad _____ _____ a truck.

5 너는 언제 일을 끝낼 수 있니?

➡ When _____ you _____ the work?

6 그것은 사실일지도 모른다.

➡ It _____ _____ true.

7 그녀는 그 답을 알지도 모른다.

➡ She _____ _____ the answer.

8 그는 오늘 안 올지도 모른다.

➡ He _____ _____ _____ today.

9 신문을 읽어도 될까요?

➡ May _____ _____ the newspaper?

10 당신이 원한다면 이곳에 머물러도 좋습니다.

➡ You _____ _____ here if you want to.

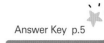

B 주어진 말을 이용하여 우리말을 영어로 바꿔 쓰세요.

1 그녀는 중국어를 할 수 있다. (Chinese)

→ <u>She can speak Chinese.</u>

2 나는 그 상자를 혼자 운반할 수 있다. (carry, by myself)

→ _____

3 너는 영어로 된 노래를 부를 수 있니? (in English)

→ _____

4 나는 이 글자들을 읽을 수 없다. (these letters)

→ _____

5 그는 다음 달에 이사를 갈지도 모른다. (move)

→ _____

6 너는 그것을 믿지 않을지도 모른다. (believe)

→ _____

7 나는 이번 여름에 태국에 갈지도 모른다. (Thailand, this summer)

→ _____

8 당신은 퇴원해도 좋습니다. (leave the hospital)

→ _____

9 화장실을 써도 될까요? (may, the bathroom)

→ _____

10 당신은 이 지역에 주차할 수 없습니다. (park in this area)

→ _____

TIP 1

can은 '~할 수 있다'라는 의미로 능력과 가능을 나타내요.

e.g.
- I can swim.
- He can't run fast.
- Can you help me?

TIP 2

may는 '~일지도 모른다'라는 약한 추측과, '~해도 좋다'라는 허락의 의미를 나타내요. 단, 의문문에서는 I, we만 주어로 사용할 수 있어요.

e.g.
- May you leave now?
 (×)
- May I/we leave now?
 (○)

WRAP UP

A Grammar ( )안에서 알맞은 것을 고르세요.

1 Alex (can, can't) drive a car. He has a driver's license.

2 He (can, can't) help you. He's very busy now.

3 (Can, May) you show me your holiday photos?

4 She (can't, may not) be at home, but I'm not sure.

5 We (may, may not) go out tonight. It's too cold.

6 Students may (use, using) the computers in the library.

7 May (I, you) have some ice cream, please?

B Writing 주어진 말을 이용하여 우리말을 영어로 바꿔 쓰세요.

1 그녀는 영작을 잘할 수 있다. (write English)

→ She can write English well.

2 너는 복도에서 뛸 수 없다. (in the hallway)

→ _____

3 내일 우리 집에 올 수 있어? (to my house)

→ _____

4 그는 언젠가 의사가 될지도 모른다. (become, someday)

→ _____

5 당신의 여권을 봐도 될까요? (may, passport)

→ _____

C 내신 대비 질문을 읽고, 알맞은 답을 고르세요.

1 밑줄 친 부분의 뜻이 <u>다른</u> 하나는?

① He <u>may</u> buy a new car.

② They <u>may</u> know my name.

③ It <u>may</u> rain this afternoon.

④ You <u>may</u> come in if you want to.

2 우리말을 영어로 바르게 옮긴 것은?

> 저의 부탁 좀 들어 주시겠어요?

① Can I do you a favor?

② May I do you a favor?

③ Can you do me a favor?

④ May you do me a favor?

개념 Review

아래 빈칸을 채우면서 개념을 다시 한번 익혀보세요.

❶ Can

☑ 조동사 can은 '~할 수 있다'라는 의미로 **❶**　　　　　이나 **❷**　　　　　을 나타내요. 이때 can과 같은 조동사 뒤에는 반드시 **❸**　　　　　이 와요.

☑ can의 부정문은 **❹**　　　　　또는 **❺**　　　　　를 사용하고, 의문문은 can을 주어 앞으로 보내서 만들 수 있어요.

❷ May

☑ 조동사 may는 '~일지도 모른다'라는 약한 **❻**　　　　　의 의미를 나타내고 부정문은 **❼**　　　　　을 사용해요.

☑ may는 '~해도 좋다'라는 허락의 의미를 나타내기도 해요. '~해도 좋습니까?'라고 상대방에게 허락을 구할 때는 '**❽**　　　　　~?'로 물을 수 있어요.

UNIT 02 Must / Have to

1 Must

You **must not** park here.

She **must** be a tourist.

의미		
의무 (~해야 한다)	They **must** follow the rules. You **must not** talk in class. I **mustn't** forget Ann's birthday.	그들은 그 규칙들을 따라야 한다. 너는 수업 시간에 떠들면 안 된다. 나는 Ann의 생일을 잊어서는 안 된다.
강한 추측 (~임에 틀림없다)	She **must** feel tired. He **must not** be hungry. That **mustn't** be true.	그녀는 틀림없이 피곤할 것이다. 그는 틀림없이 배가 고프지 않을 것이다. 그것은 틀림없이 사실이 아닐 것이다.

☑ 조동사 must는 '~해야 한다'라는 **의무**를 나타내요. 부정형 must not은 '~해서는 안 된다'라는 **금지**를 나타내요.

☑ must는 '~임에 틀림없다'라는 **강한 추측**을 나타내기도 해요.

☑ must not은 줄여서 **mustn't**로 쓸 수 있어요.

PRACTICE 1 문장 완성하기

❶ 우리는 지금 가야 한다. → We ___must___ ___go___ now.

❷ 너는 늦으면 안 된다. → You _____ _____ _____ late.

❸ 그녀는 틀림없이 집에 있을 것이다. → She _____ _____ at home.

❹ 그는 틀림없이 Sam을 모를 것이다. → He _____ _____ _____ Sam.

2 Have to

She **has to** wear glasses.

He **doesn't have to** wear a coat.

문장의 종류		
긍정문 (~해야 한다)	I **have to** get up early. He **has to** go to the dentist.	나는 일찍 일어나야 한다. 그는 치과에 가야 한다.
부정문 (~할 필요가 없다)	You **don't have to** do it now. She **doesn't have to** hurry.	너는 그것을 지금 할 필요가 없다. 그녀는 서두를 필요가 없다.
의문문 (~해야 하나요?)	**Do** we **have to** take a taxi? **Does** he **have to** go downtown?	우리는 택시를 타야 하나요? 그는 시내에 가야 하나요?

☑ **have to**도 must와 같은 의미로 '~해야 한다'라는 **의무**를 나타내요. 주어가 3인칭 단수(he / she / it)일 때는 **has to**를 써요.

☑ 부정형은 **don't / doesn't have to**로 '~할 필요가 없다'를 의미하고, 의문문은 「**Do / Does + 주어 + have to + 동사원형 ~?**」
으로 나타내요.

PRACTICE 2 문장 완성하기

❶ 그녀는 그 약을 복용해야 한다. ➡ She ____has____ ____to____ take the medicine.

❷ 그는 금연을 해야 한다. ➡ He _____ _____ stop smoking.

❸ 너는 말할 필요가 없다. ➡ You _____ _____ _____ talk.

❹ 제가 거기에 가야 하나요? ➡ _____ I _____ _____ go there?

A 주어진 문장을 have to를 이용한 문장으로 바꿔 쓰세요.

1 You must wear your seatbelt.

→ You have to wear your seatbelt.

2 She must clean the bathroom.

→

3 You must listen to your teacher.

→

4 He must take out the garbage.

→

5 They must pass the exam to graduate.

→

6 You must stop at the red light.

→

7 We must buy some milk.

→

8 I must visit my friend in the hospital.

→

9 He must do some exercise.

→

10 You must fill out this form.

→

WORDS seatbelt 안전벨트   bathroom 욕실   take out the garbage 쓰레기를 버리다   graduate 졸업하다
visit someone in the hospital ~의 병문안을 가다   fill out ~을 작성하다   form (문서의) 양식

B ( ) 안에서 알맞은 것을 고르세요.

1 The sun is very strong. I (must, don't have to) wear sunglasses.

2 I like Sundays because I (must, don't have to) go to school.

3 Do we (must, have to) get up early tomorrow?

4 You (mustn't, don't have to) swim here. It's very deep.

5 The house is on fire! You (mustn't, have to) call the fire department.

6 Paul stayed up all night. He (must, has to) feel tired.

7 You (must, don't have to) stop smoking. It's harmful.

8 I (mustn't, have to) forget to call Jane. It's her birthday.

9 You (mustn't, have to) yell at people. It's very rude.

10 He's a millionaire. He (must, doesn't have to) work.

11 John (mustn't, has to) see a doctor. His back is hurt.

12 The book sells well. It (must, has to) be interesting.

13 He's not answering the phone. He (must not, doesn't have to) be at home.

14 Amy has many friends. She (mustn't, has to) be lonely.

15 How long does he (must, have to) stay in the hospital?

 WORDS   deep 깊은   **on fire** 불이 붙은, 불이 난   **fire department** 소방서   **stay up** 안 자다, 깨어 있다
smoking 흡연   **harmful** 해로운   **forget** 잊다   **yell** 소리 지르다   **rude** 무례한   **millionaire** 백만장자
back 등   **hurt** 다친   **lonely** 외로운

A 우리말과 같은 뜻이 되도록 빈칸에 알맞은 말을 쓰세요.

1 나는 그에게 사실을 말해야 한다.

➡ I <u>must</u> <u>tell</u> him the truth.

2 너는 정크 푸드를 먹는 것을 그만두어야 한다.

➡ You _____ _____ eating junk food.

3 이 안에서 담배를 피우면 안 된다.

➡ You _____ _____ _____ in here.

4 그녀는 좋은 친구임이 틀림없다.

➡ She _____ _____ a good friend.

5 그들은 그 소식을 알지 못하는 것이 틀림없다.

➡ They _____ _____ _____ the news.

6 모든 학생들은 교복을 입어야 한다.

➡ All students _____ _____ _____ school uniforms.

7 우리는 서두를 필요가 없다.

➡ We _____ _____ _____ hurry.

8 그는 지금 떠나야 합니까?

➡ _____ he _____ _____ leave now?

9 제가 얼마나 오래 기다려야 하나요?

➡ How long _____ I _____ _____ _____ ?

10 우리는 하루에 세 번 양치질을 해야 한다.

➡ We _____ _____ _____ our teeth three times a day.

B 주어진 말을 이용하여 우리말을 영어로 바꿔 쓰세요.

1 나는 안경을 써야 한다. (glasses)

➡   I must[have to] wear glasses.

2 나는 그 책을 반납해야 한다. (return)

➡

3 동물들에게 먹이를 주면 안 됩니다. (feed, the animals)

➡

4 네 친구의 숙제를 베끼면 안 된다. (copy, your friend's homework)

➡

5 그것은 틀림없이 매우 신날 것이다. (very exciting)

➡

6 그녀는 몸이 좋지 않은 것이 틀림없다. (feel well)

➡

7 학생들은 교실을 청소해야 한다. (the classroom)

➡

8 너는 걱정할 필요 없어. (worry)

➡

9 우리는 지하철을 타야 하니? (take the subway)

➡

10 그는 다음 주말에 일해야 하니? (work next weekend)

➡

must는 '~해야 한다'라는 의무와 '~임에 틀림없다'라는 강한 추측의 의미를 나타내요.

e.g.
- You must do your homework. (의무)
- That must be true. (강한 추측)

must와 have to는 둘 다 긍정문에서 '~해야 한다'라는 의무를 나타내지만, 부정문에서는 뜻이 달라지므로 주의해야 해요.

e.g.
- You must[have to] go. (의무)
- You mustn't go. (금지)
- You don't have to go. (불필요)

WRAP UP

A Grammar 밑줄 친 부분을 바르게 고치세요.

1 You must <u>obeys</u> your parents. → <u>obey</u>

2 Sometimes he <u>have to</u> work on the weekend. → ___

3 You <u>must not to</u> be late for school. → ___

4 She has five dogs. She <u>has to</u> like dogs. → ___

5 You <u>don't must</u> talk during an exam. → ___

6 You <u>must not</u> do it now. You can do it later. → ___

7 <u>Do I must</u> move this table? → ___

B Writing 주어진 말을 이용하여 우리말을 영어로 바꿔 쓰세요.

1 당신은 좀 쉬어야 해요. (get some rest)
→ You must[have to] get some rest.

2 잔디 위를 걸어 다니면 안 됩니다. (on a grass)
→ ___

3 그는 액션 영화를 좋아하는 것이 틀림없어. (action movies)
→ ___

4 당신은 입장권을 구입할 필요가 없다. (buy a ticket)
→ ___

5 우리가 얼마나 오래 그 버스를 기다려야 하나요? (how long, wait for)
→ ___

C 내신 대비 질문을 읽고, 알맞은 답을 고르세요.

1 밑줄 친 부분의 뜻이 다른 하나는?

① I <u>must</u> keep my promise.

② You <u>must</u> be on time for work.

③ She <u>must</u> take care of the baby.

④ He <u>must</u> be tired after the long walk.

2 우리말을 영어로 바르게 옮긴 것은?

> 당신은 기차를 갈아탈 필요가 없다.

① You must not change trains.

② You have to not change trains.

③ You have not to change trains.

④ You don't have to change trains.

개념 Review

아래 빈칸을 채우면서 개념을 다시 한번 익혀보세요.

① Must

☑ 조동사 must는 '~해야 한다'라는 ❶ _____ 를 나타내요. 부정형 must not은 '~해서는 안 된다' 라는 ❷ _____ 를 나타내요.

☑ must는 '~임에 틀림없다'라는 ❸ _____ 을 나타내기도 해요.

☑ must not은 줄여서 ❹ _____ 로 쓸 수 있어요.

② Have to

☑ have to도 must와 같은 의미로 '~해야 한다'라는 ❺ _____ 를 나타내요. 주어가 3인칭 단수 (he / she / it)일 때는 has to를 써요.

☑ 부정형은 don't / doesn't have to로 '~할 필요가 없다'를 의미하고, 의문문은 「Do / Does + 주어 + have to + ❻ _____ ~?」으로 나타내요.

[01-02] 대화의 빈칸에 알맞은 말을 고르시오.

01

A What are you going to do tonight?

B I'm not sure. I _____ go to the movies.

① may

② must

③ can't

④ have to

02

A Is it raining outside?

B No, it isn't. You _____ take your umbrella.

① may

② have to

③ mustn't

④ don't have to

03 밑줄 친 부분과 바꿔 쓸 수 있는 것은?

You <u>must</u> turn off your cell phone during the movie.

① can

② may

③ have to

④ don't have to

04 빈칸에 들어갈 말로 <u>어색한</u> 것은?

The rumor _____ be true.

① may

② must

③ has to

④ may not

05 빈칸에 들어갈 말이 순서대로 바르게 짝지어진 것은?

A I _____ lose weight.

B Then you _____ eat so much food.

① can't – may

② may not – can

③ have to – mustn't

④ must – don't have to

서술형

[06-07] 우리말과 같은 뜻이 되도록 빈칸에 알맞은 말을 쓰시오.

06

제가 벌금을 내야만 하나요?

→ _____ I _____ _____ pay a fine?

07

우리는 이 방에서 바다를 볼 수 있다.

→ We _____ _____ the ocean from this room.

[08-09] 밑줄 친 부분의 뜻이 <u>다른</u> 하나를 고르시오.

08 ① It <u>may</u> snow tonight.

② We <u>may</u> sell our house.

③ The bus <u>may</u> go downtown.

④ <u>May</u> I have your name, please?

09 ① He <u>must not</u> eat sweets.

② The movie <u>must not</u> be fun.

③ You <u>must not</u> drive too fast.

④ I <u>must not</u> spend too much money.

[10-11] 다음 중 <u>틀린</u> 문장을 고르시오.

10 ① Can you play chess?

② Do I have to leave now?

③ May you open the door?

④ Does she have to clean the kitchen?

11 ① It may be his mistake.

② They must to do the work.

③ He can cook Chinese dishes.

④ She has to go to the supermarket.

[12-13] 우리말을 영어로 바르게 옮긴 것을 고르시오.

12
> 그 바지는 나에게 맞지 않을지도 모른다.

① The pants cannot fit me.

② The pants may not fit me.

③ The pants must not fit me.

④ The pants don't have to fit me.

13
> 그 축제는 틀림없이 재미있을 것이다.

① The festival can be fun.

② The festival may be fun.

③ The festival must be fun.

④ The festival has to be fun.

서술형

[14-15] 주어진 말을 이용하여 우리말을 영어로 바꿔 쓰시오.

14
> 너는 다시는 지각을 해서는 안 된다.
> (be late, again)

➡ _____

15
> Mike는 치과에 갈 필요가 없다.
> (go to the dentist)

➡ _____

03

비교

학습목표

1 원급, 비교급, 최상급의 규칙 변화와 불규칙 변화를 알아봐요.

2 비교급과 최상급의 다양한 표현을 익히고, 비교급을 강조하는 방법을 알아봐요.

비교급과 최상급: 규칙 변화

1 비교급과 최상급 만들기

a **big** gift box

a **bigger** gift box

the **biggest** gift box

형용사/부사의 형태	원급	비교급	최상급
1음절 단어	long	long**er**	long**est**
-e로 끝나는 단어	nice	nice**r**	nice**st**
단모음+단자음으로 끝나는 단어	sad	sad**der**	sad**dest**
-y로 끝나는 단어	early	earl**ier**	earl**iest**
대부분의 2음절 이상 단어	beautiful	**more** beautiful	**most** beautiful

☑ 형용사나 부사에 **-er** 또는 **more**를 붙이면 '더 ~한 / 하게'란 뜻의 **비교급**이 돼요.

☑ 형용사나 부사에 **-est** 또는 **most**를 붙이면 '가장 ~한 / 하게'란 뜻의 **최상급**이 돼요. 최상급 앞에는 보통 the를 붙여요.

PRACTICE 1 비교급과 최상급 만들기 (규칙 변화)

❶ slow   _____slower_____   _____slowest_____

❷ hot   _____   _____

❸ pretty   _____   _____

❹ important   _____   _____

2 비교급과 최상급 표현

I am **taller than** my sister.

My dad is **the tallest** person **in** my family.

비교급＋than	A cheetah can run **faster than** a lion. 치타는 사자보다 더 빨리 달릴 수 있다. My chair is **more comfortable than** yours. 내 의자는 너의 것보다 더 편안하다.
the＋최상급 ~ in/of	That church is **the oldest** building **in** town. 저 교회는 시내에서 가장 오래된 건물이다. The cake was **the most delicious** dessert **of** all. 케이크가 모든 것 중에서도 가장 맛있는 후식이었다.

☑ 「비교급＋than」은 '~보다 더 …한 / 하게'를 의미해요.

☑ 「the＋최상급 ~ in / of」는 '~에서 가장 …한 / 하게'를 의미해요. 최상급 뒤에는 in이나 of를 써서 범위를 나타낼 수 있어요.

PRACTICE 2 알맞은 말 고르기

❶ Bananas are (sweeter, sweetest) than lemons.

❷ August is the (hotter, hottest) month of the year.

❸ The princess is (more beautiful, most beautiful) than the witch.

❹ That is the (more expensive, most expensive) restaurant in this town.

A 주어진 단어의 비교급과 최상급을 쓰세요.

1	old	older	oldest
2	short		
3	big		
4	fast		
5	large		
6	hot		
7	cheap		
8	easy		
9	wide		
10	cold		
11	heavy		
12	thin		
13	useful		
14	expensive		
15	attractive		

WORDS cheap (값이) 싼 thin 얇은; 마른 useful 유용한 expensive 비싼 attractive 매력적인

B 주어진 단어를 비교급과 최상급 중 알맞은 형태로 고쳐 쓰세요.

1 My dad wants a _____bigger_____ car. (big)

2 This dress is _____ than that one. (nice)

3 What is the _____ building in the world? (tall)

4 The mountain is _____ than the hill. (high)

5 Today is the _____ day of my life. (lucky)

6 The subway is _____ than the bus. (fast)

7 This week is _____ than last week. (hot)

8 Fruit is _____ than junk food. (healthy)

9 February is the _____ month of the year. (short)

10 Bicycles are _____ than cars. (cheap)

11 She is the _____ girl in the class. (pretty)

12 My dad is the _____ person in my family. (old)

13 The restaurant is _____ than usual. (busy)

14 Music is the _____ subject to me. (interesting)

15 Ben is _____ than his classmates. (intelligent)

 WORDS hill 언덕 lucky 운이 좋은 subway 지하철 healthy 건강한; 건강에 좋은 junk food 정크푸드
busy 붐비는; 바쁜 usual 평상시의 subject 과목 intelligent 지적인 classmate 반 친구

영작 술술

A 우리말과 같은 뜻이 되도록 빈칸에 알맞은 말을 쓰세요.

1 Jimmy는 Tom보다 더 게으르다.

→ Jimmy is ____lazier____ ____than____ Tom.

2 나는 평소보다 더 일찍 일어났다.

→ I got up _____ _____ usual.

3 장미는 튤립보다 더 아름답다.

→ Roses are _____ _____ _____ tulips.

4 그 목걸이는 그 팔찌보다 더 비싸다.

→ The necklace is _____ _____ _____ the bracelet.

5 Jane은 그 시험에서 가장 높은 점수를 받았다.

→ Jane got _____ _____ score on the test.

6 1월은 일년 중 가장 추운 달이다.

→ January is _____ _____ month of the year.

7 나는 우리 식구 중 가장 어린 사람이다.

→ I am _____ _____ person in my family.

8 이것은 그 동네에서 가장 오래된 건물이다.

→ This is _____ _____ building in the neighborhood.

9 축구는 이탈리아에서 가장 인기 있는 스포츠이다.

→ Soccer is _____ _____ _____ sport in Italy.

10 이것은 공원에서 가장 큰 나무이다.

→ This is _____ _____ tree in the park.

B 주어진 말을 이용하여 우리말을 영어로 바꿔 쓰세요.

1 백두산은 한라산보다 더 높다. (Mt. Baekdu, than, Mt. Halla)

➡ Mt. Baekdu is higher than Mt. Halla.

2 오늘은 어제보다 더 따뜻하다. (today, warm)

➡ _____

3 Tina는 그녀의 언니보다 더 날씬하다. (thin)

➡ _____

4 건강은 돈보다 더 중요하다. (good health, important)

➡ _____

5 중국어는 영어보다 더 어렵다. (Chinese, difficult, English)

➡ _____

6 오늘은 내 인생에서 가장 슬픈 날이다. (today, of my life)

➡ _____

7 나일강은 세계에서 가장 긴 강이다. (the Nile, in the world)

➡ _____

8 서울은 한국에서 가장 큰 도시이다. (large, in Korea)

➡ _____

9 그는 그 반에서 가장 잘생긴 소년이다. (handsome, in the class)

➡ _____

10 바흐는 역사상 가장 위대한 음악가이다. (Bach, musician, in history)

➡ _____

TIP 1

대부분의 형용사와 부사는 er, est를 붙여 비교급, 최상급을 만들고, 2음절 이상인 단어는 more, most를 사용해요.

e.g.
- strong (원급)
  stronger (비교급)
  strongest (최상급)
- expensive (원급)
  more expensive (비교급)
  most expensive (최상급)

TIP 2

최상급 앞에는 보통 the를 붙여요.

e.g.
- She is the tallest girl of all.

WRAP UP

A Grammar 밑줄 친 부분을 바르게 고치세요.

1 Math is <u>easyer</u> than English. → easier

2 Your room is <u>more clean</u> than mine. →

3 Summer is the <u>hotest</u> season of all. →

4 My mom is <u>oldest</u> than my dad. →

5 She is the <u>most fast</u> runner of all. →

6 He is the <u>wiser</u> man in the town. →

7 I saw <u>a longest hotdog</u> in the world. →

B Writing 주어진 말을 이용하여 우리말을 영어로 바꿔 쓰세요.

1 자전거는 오토바이보다 더 안전하다. (bicycles, safe, motorcycles)

  → Bicycles are safer than motorcycles.

2 John은 Mike보다 더 뚱뚱하다. (fat)

  →

3 시골은 도시보다 더 평화롭다. (the country, peaceful, the city)

  →

4 Amy는 그 반에서 키가 가장 작은 소녀이다. (short, in the class)

  →

5 내 일기장은 나에게 가장 중요한 것이다. (diary, important thing, to me)

  →

C 내신 대비 질문을 읽고, 알맞은 답을 고르세요.

1 비교급과 최상급이 잘못 짝지어진 것은?

① big – biger – bigest

② neat – neater – neatest

③ heavy – heavier – heaviest

④ useful – more useful – most useful

2 우리말을 영어로 바르게 옮긴 것은?

> 태양은 달보다 더 밝다.

① The sun is bright than the moon.

② The sun is brighter than the moon.

③ The sun is more bright than the moon.

④ The sun is the most bright than the moon.

개념 Review

아래 빈칸을 채우면서 개념을 다시 한번 익혀보세요.

❶ 비교급과 최상급 만들기 (규칙 변화)

☑ 형용사나 부사에 ❶ _____ 또는 ❷ _____ 을 붙이면 '더 ~한 / 하게'란 뜻의 비교급이 돼요.

☑ 형용사나 부사에 ❸ _____ 또는 ❹ _____ 를 붙이면 '가장 ~한 / 하게'란 뜻의 최상급이 돼요. 최상급 앞에는 보통 the를 붙여요.

❷ 비교급과 최상급 표현

☑ 「❺ _____ +than」은 '~보다 더 …한 / 하게'를 의미해요.

☑ 「the + ❻ _____ ~ in / of」는 '~에서 가장 …한 / 하게'를 의미해요. 최상급 뒤에는 in이나 of를 써서 범위를 나타낼 수 있어요.

UNIT 02 비교급과 최상급: 불규칙 변화

1 비교급과 최상급 만들기

Lucy got a **good** grade.

Ann got a **better** grade.

Joanne got the **best** grade.

원급	비교급	최상급	
good / well	better	best	I feel **better** than yesterday. 나는 어제보다 기분이 더 좋다.
bad	worse	worst	My grade is **worse** than yours. 내 점수는 너의 것보다 더 나쁘다.
many / much	more	most	Bob has the **most** books of all. Bob은 가장 많은 책을 갖고 있다.
little	less	least	I have **less** money than you. 나는 너보다 더 적은 돈을 갖고 있다.

☑ 일부 형용사와 부사들은 비교급과 최상급이 불규칙하게 변화하므로 주의해야 해요.

PRACTICE 1 비교급과 최상급 만들기 (불규칙 변화)

❶ good   _____better_____   _____best_____

❷ bad   _____   _____

❸ many   _____   _____

❹ little   _____   _____

2 비교급과 최상급 표현

The watermelon is **much bigger** than the apple.

My English is getting **better and better.**

much + 비교급	Katie is **much taller** than Robert. Katie가 Robert보다 훨씬 더 키가 크다.
비교급 + and + 비교급	It is getting **warmer and warmer.** (날씨가) 점점 더 따뜻해진다. This book is getting **more and more interesting.** 이 책은 점점 더 재미있어진다.
one of the + 최상급 + 복수 명사	Paul is **one of the best players** on the team. Paul은 그 팀에서 가장 뛰어난 선수들 중 한 명이다.

☑ 비교급을 강조할 때는 비교급 앞에 **much**를 사용하고 '훨씬 더 ~한'을 의미해요.

☑ 「비교급 + and + 비교급」은 '점점 더 ~한'의 의미로 상태의 변화를 나타내요.

☑ 「one of the + 최상급 + 복수 명사」는 '가장 ~한 … 중의 하나'를 의미해요.

PRACTICE 2 알맞은 말 고르기

❶ His work is getting (good and good, ⬭better and better⬭).

❷ Buses are (many, much) cheaper than taxis.

❸ He is one of the (richer, richest) men in the world.

❹ These days, (more and more, most and most) people are learning Korean.

 문법 쏙쏙

A ( ) 안에서 알맞은 것을 고르세요.

1 Paul is a (good, better, best) student.

2 Daniel has (many, more, most) toys than Betty.

3 It was the (bad, worse, worst) week of my life.

4 Susan eats (little, less, least) than Tom.

5 Tom is a (good, better, best) driver than Brian.

6 The weather is (good, better, best) than yesterday.

7 We spent very (little, less, least) money last month.

8 My handwriting is bad, but Tara's is (bad, worse, worst).

9 Who is the (good, better, best) worker at the company?

10 Peter can run (little, less, least) fast than Mike.

11 We chose the (little, less, least) expensive hotel in the city.

12 This red apple tastes (good, better, best) than the green one.

13 The milk in the refrigerator is (bad, worse, worst).

14 The dress is the (little, less, least) attractive of the three.

15 I made the (many, more, most) mistakes of all the team members.

 WORDS spend (돈을) 쓰다; (시간을) 보내다   handwriting 필체   company 회사   refrigerator 냉장고
attractive 매력적인   mistake 실수

B 주어진 말을 바르게 배열하여 문장을 완성하세요.

1 much / feel / than / yesterday / I / better / .
→ ___I feel much better than yesterday.___

2 me / older / is / much / than / my grandfather / .
→ _____

3 mine / your room / cleaner / is / much / than / .
→ _____

4 silver / more / is / gold / than / expensive / much / .
→ _____

5 is getting / the balloon / and / bigger / bigger / .
→ _____

6 more / exciting / the game / and / more / got / .
→ _____

7 electric cars / and / people / more / more / are buying / .
→ _____

8 of the year / the film / the best movies / one of / is / .
→ _____

9 one of / it is / the largest cities / in the country / .
→ _____

10 the most difficult / one of / Arabic is / languages / .
→ _____

WORDS mine 나의 것 gold 금 silver 은 balloon 풍선 exciting 흥미진진한, 신나는 electric car 전기차
Arabic 아랍어 language 언어

영작 술술

A 우리말과 같은 뜻이 되도록 빈칸에 알맞은 말을 쓰세요.

1 Sarah는 Kelly보다 더 많은 책을 가지고 있다.

→ Sarah has ___more___ ___books___ ___than___ Kelly.

2 나는 양식보다 한식을 더 좋아한다.

→ I like Korean food _____ _____ Western food.

3 너희 학교에서 가장 좋은 선생님이 누구시니?

→ Who is _____ _____ _____ at your school?

4 그날은 내 인생의 최악의 날이었다.

→ It was _____ _____ _____ of my life.

5 그것은 그 상점에서 가장 덜 비싼 신발이다.

→ Those are _____ _____ _____ shoes in the shop.

6 중국은 세계에서 가장 많은 사람들을 보유하고 있다.

→ China has _____ _____ _____ in the world.

7 그의 새 차는 그의 이전의 차보다 훨씬 더 빠르다.

→ His new car is _____ _____ _____ his old one.

8 이 영화는 책보다 훨씬 더 흥미롭다.

→ This movie is _____ _____ _____ than the book.

9 내 양말의 구멍이 점점 더 커지고 있다.

→ The hole in my sock is getting _____ _____ _____ .

10 그것은 그 식당에서 가장 인기 있는 메뉴들 중 하나이다.

→ It is _____ _____ _____ _____ _____ menu items
at the restaurant.

B 주어진 말을 이용하여 우리말을 영어로 바꿔 쓰세요.

1 David는 Ryan보다 더 나은 선수이다. (player)

➡ ___David is a better player than Ryan.___

2 Ann은 그 반에서 가장 좋은 성적을 받았다. (get, grade, in the class)

➡ _____

3 그는 그 셋 중에서 가장 노래를 못하는 사람이다. (singer, of the three)

➡ _____

4 Sally는 그녀의 언니보다 훨씬 더 외향적이다. (outgoing)

➡ _____

5 내 용돈은 일주일에 20달러 이하이다. (allowance, a week)

➡ _____

6 나는 평소보다 훨씬 더 늦게 잤다. (go to bed, usual)

➡ _____

7 그는 그 반에서 가장 인기 없는 학생이다. (popular, in the class)

➡ _____

8 그녀의 건강은 점점 더 나빠지고 있다. (get)

➡ _____

9 그는 점점 더 유명해졌다. (become, famous)

➡ _____

10 그것은 가장 인상적인 연설들 중 하나였다. (impressive speech)

➡ _____

TIP 1

비교급을 강조할 때는 much를 사용하며 '훨씬'이라는 뜻을 나타내요.

e.g.
- Tom is much taller than Mike.

TIP 2

'가장 ~한 … 중의 하나'는 「one of the+최상급+복수 명사」로 나타내며, 이때 최상급 뒤에는 항상 복수 명사가 와요.

e.g.
- one of the biggest city (x)
- one of the biggest cities (o)

WRAP UP

A Grammar 밑줄 친 부분을 바르게 고치세요.

1 Who is the <u>better</u> singer in the choir? ➡ _best_

2 Brian is a <u>good</u> cook than Betty. ➡ _____

3 He is the <u>worse</u> dresser of the three. ➡ _____

4 We had <u>most</u> snow than last year. ➡ _____

5 Your dress is <u>much nice</u> than mine. ➡ _____

6 Laptops are getting <u>thin and thin</u>. ➡ _____

7 It was one of <u>the funniest movie</u>. ➡ _____

B Writing 주어진 말을 이용하여 우리말을 영어로 바꿔 쓰세요.

1 그녀는 그녀의 언니보다 덜 상냥하다. (friendly)

➡ _She is less friendly than her sister._

2 나는 반에서 가장 나쁜 성적을 받았다. (get, grade, in the class)

➡ _____

3 그의 집은 우리 집보다 훨씬 더 크다. (ours)

➡ _____

4 날씨가 점점 더 추워지고 있다. (the weather, get)

➡ _____

5 그 책은 가장 잘 팔리는 책들 중 하나이다. (best seller)

➡ _____

C 내신 대비 질문을 읽고, 알맞은 답을 고르세요.

1 다음 중 **틀린** 문장은?

① Traffic is worse than usual.

② This job is better than my old one.

③ I bought the less expensive shoes in the shop.

④ The bakery has the best cheesecake in the city.

2 우리말을 영어로 바르게 옮긴 것은?

> 그는 세계에서 가장 위대한 과학자들 중 하나이다.

① He is one of the great scientists in the world.

② He is one of the greatest scientist in the world.

③ He is one of the greatest scientists in the world.

④ He is one of the most great scientists in the world.

개념 Review

아래 빈칸을 채우면서 개념을 다시 한번 익혀보세요.

❶ **비교급과 최상급 만들기 (불규칙 변화)**

☑ 일부 형용사와 부사들은 비교급과 최상급이 불규칙하게 변화하므로 주의해야 해요.

❷ **비교급과 최상급 표현**

☑ 비교급을 강조할 때는 비교급 앞에 ❶ ＿＿＿＿＿ 를 사용하고 '훨씬 더 ~한'을 의미해요.

☑ 「❷ ＿＿＿＿＿ + and + ❸ ＿＿＿＿＿」은 '점점 더 ~한'의 의미로 상태의 변화를 나타내요.

☑ 「one of the + ❹ ＿＿＿＿＿ + ❺ ＿＿＿＿＿」는 '가장 ~한 … 중의 하나'를 의미해요.

[01-02] 대화의 빈칸에 알맞은 말을 고르시오.

01

> A How was the movie?
> B It was _____ than the last one.

① interesting
② interestinger
③ most interesting
④ more interesting

02

> A The exam was not difficult.
> B Yeah, it was one of the _____ exams.

① easy
② easier
③ easiest
④ most easy

03 비교급과 최상급이 잘못 짝지어진 것은?

① good – better – best
② little – littler – littlest
③ hot – hotter – hottest
④ happy – happier – happiest

04 빈칸에 들어갈 말로 알맞은 것은?

> Australia is _____ bigger than New Zealand.

① much
② more
③ many
④ better

05 빈칸에 들어갈 말로 알맞지 <u>않은</u> 것은?

> Yesterday was the _____ day of my life.

① best
② worse
③ saddest
④ happiest

서술형

[06-07] 우리말과 같은 뜻이 되도록 빈칸에 알맞은 말을 쓰시오.

06

> 나는 태국 음식보다 이탈리아 음식을 더 좋아한다.

➡ I like Italian food _____ _____ Thai food.

07

> 점점 더 많은 사람들이 인터넷 쇼핑을 한다.

➡ _____ _____ _____ people are shopping online.

08 빈칸에 들어갈 말로 알맞은 것은?

> Tom is 170 cm tall, and Jack is 165 cm tall.
>
> Tom is _____ Jack.

① tall than   ② taller than

③ tallest than   ④ more tall than

[09-10] 다음 중 **틀린** 문장을 고르시오.

09 ① Your boots are dirtier than mine.

② Seoul is the biggest city in Korea.

③ He is smartest than other students.

④ The ring is more expensive than the watch.

10 ① This is the best restaurant in the city.

② *Cats* is one of the most popular musical.

③ Mike is much more handsome than Mark.

④ Your Spanish is getting better and better.

11 밑줄 친 부분이 올바른 것은?

① He is <u>worst dancer</u> of all.

② I'm feeling <u>more and more tired</u>.

③ Today is <u>more warm</u> than yesterday.

④ The coffee costs <u>least</u> than five dollars.

[12-13] 우리말을 영어로 바르게 옮긴 것을 고르시오.

12
> Betty는 Sally보다 더 많은 신발을 갖고 있다.

① Betty has more pairs of shoes than Sally.

② Betty has many pairs of shoes than Sally.

③ Betty has the most pairs of shoes than Sally.

④ Betty has many most pairs of shoes than Sally.

13
> 나는 점점 더 뚱뚱해지고 있다.

① I am getting fat and fat.

② I am getting more fatter.

③ I am getting fatter and fatter.

④ I am getting more and more fat.

서술형

[14-15] 주어진 말을 이용하여 우리말을 영어로 바꿔 쓰시오.

14
> 해바라기는 장미보다 더 크다.
> (sunflowers, roses)

➡ _____

15
> 그는 세계에서 가장 유명한 배우들 중 하나이다.
> (famous actor, in the world)

➡ _____

04

전치사

학습목표

1 시간의 전치사 at, in, on의 의미를 알아보고, 그 밖의 다양한 시간의 전치사들을 알아봐요.

2 장소의 전치사 in, on, under, next to의 의미를 알아보고, 그 밖의 다양한 장소 전치사들도 알아봐요.

UNIT 01 시간의 전치사

1 at / in / on

We have breakfast **at** 8 o'clock.

The shop is closed **on** Sunday.

at		in		on	
at 7 o'clock	7시에	**in** 2023	2023년에	**on** Monday	월요일에
at noon	정오에	**in** January	1월에	**on** January 10	1월 10일에
at night	밤에	**in** summer	여름에	**on** Children's Day	어린이날에
at midnight	자정에	**in** the morning	아침에	**on** Friday night	금요일 밤에
				on the weekend	주말에

☑ **전치사**는 명사 앞에서 시간이나 장소 등을 나타내주는 말이에요.

☑ **at, in, on**은 대표적인 시간 전치사로, **at**은 구체적인 시각, 특정한 시점, **in**은 연도, 월, 계절 등 비교적 긴 시간, **on**은 요일, 날짜, 특정한 날 앞에 사용해요.

PRACTICE 1 알맞은 시간 전치사 넣기

❶ ___in___ August

❷ _____ 7:30

❸ _____ Thursday

❹ _____ winter

❺ _____ the afternoon

❻ _____ 2022

❼ _____ Sunday morning

❽ _____ bedtime

2 기타 시간의 전치사

They are doing the dishes **after** dinner.

The shop is open **from** 6:00 a.m. **to** 3:00 p.m.

전치사	의미				
before	~ 전에	**before** class	수업 전에	**before** lunch	점심 전에
after	~ 후에	**after** school	방과 후에	**after** work	퇴근 후에
from ~ to...	~부터 ...까지	**from** 7:00 **to** 8:00	7시부터 8시까지		
for+기간	~ 동안	**for** a week	일주일 동안	**for** two hours	2시간 동안
during+명사	~ 동안, ~ 중에	**during** vacation	방학 동안	**during** the exam	시험 중에
until	~까지	**until** 10 o'clock	10시까지	**until** Friday	금요일까지

☑ 시간을 나타내는 전치사에는 **before, after, from ~ to..., for, during, until** 등도 있어요.

☑ for와 during은 모두 '~ 동안'을 의미하지만, **for** 뒤에는 **숫자로 된 기간**이, during 뒤에는 **특정 기간을 나타내는 명사**가 와요.

PRACTICE 2 알맞은 시간 전치사 넣기

❶ 저녁 식사 후에   →   <u> after </u>   dinner

❷ 월요일부터 금요일까지   →   <u>   </u>   Monday <u>   </u>   Friday

❸ 7월까지   →   <u>   </u>   July

❹ 3일 동안   →   <u>   </u>   three days

A 빈칸에 at, in, on 중에서 알맞은 전치사를 골라 쓰세요.

1   Julie was born _____in_____ 2012.

2   The movie starts _____ 12:30.

3   The music festival begins _____ October 12.

4   Leaves change color _____ fall.

5   My father goes to work _____ 8 o'clock.

6   John always gets up early _____ the morning.

7   Children like having snowball fights _____ winter.

8   Do you go to school _____ Saturday?

9   The students have lunch _____ noon.

10 My mother's birthday is _____ September.

11 What do you usually do _____ the weekend?

12 I always do my homework _____ the evening.

13 The accident happened _____ Monday afternoon.

14 You can see many beautiful flowers _____ spring.

15 My dad gave me a present _____ my birthday.

WORDS   **October** 10월   **leaf** (나뭇)잎   **fall** 가을   **snowball fight** 눈싸움   **noon** 정오, 낮 12시   **September** 9월
accident 사고   **happen** 발생하다, 일어나다   **spring** 봄

B ( ) 안에서 알맞은 전치사를 고르세요.

1 The child cried (for, until) almost two hours.

2 Paul went to school (at, after) breakfast.

3 My friend fell asleep (during, on) the movie.

4 They lived in Chicago from 2020 (to, after) 2022.

5 She took a nap (for, during) thirty minutes.

6 Jack studied hard (before, from) the exam.

7 We waited for a bus (for, from) half an hour.

8 Owls and bats sleep (during, on) the day.

9 He will stay in London (during, until) next Friday.

10 The second train leaves ten minutes (after, in) the first one.

11 I lived with my grandparents (for, in) ten years.

12 The lights went out (for, during) the storm.

13 Tom didn't get home (until, for) 10 o'clock.

14 The mall is open (from, until) 10:00 a.m. to 8:00 p.m.

15 We visited a lot of interesting places (for, during) our holiday.

 WORDS fall asleep 잠들다   take a nap 낮잠을 자다   owl 올빼미, 부엉이   bat 박쥐   day 낮; 하루; 요일
light (전깃)불, 전등   go out (불·전깃불이) 꺼지다, 나가다   storm 폭풍, 폭풍우   holiday 휴가; 휴일

영작 술술

A 우리말과 같은 뜻이 되도록 빈칸에 알맞은 말을 쓰세요.

1 그 건물은 2019년에 지어졌다.

→ The building was built ___in___ ___2019___ .

2 토요일 1시에 만나자.

→ Let's meet _____ 1 o'clock _____ Saturday.

3 그녀는 종종 주말에 쇼핑하러 간다.

→ She often goes shopping _____ _____ _____ .

4 나는 점심 식사 후에 항상 산책을 한다.

→ I always take a walk _____ _____ .

5 그들은 10시까지 통화를 했다.

→ They talked on the phone _____ _____ _____ .

6 그는 9시 이전에 학교에 도착했다.

→ He arrived at school _____ _____ _____ .

7 우리는 낮 동안 일하고 밤에 잠을 잔다.

→ We work _____ the day and sleep _____ _____ .

8 우리는 10분 동안 쉬었다.

→ We took a break _____ _____ _____ .

9 그 미술관은 월요일부터 금요일까지 문을 연다.

→ The art museum is open _____ Monday _____ Friday.

10 너는 수업 중에 시끄럽게 떠들어서는 안 된다.

→ You cannot talk loudly _____ _____ .

B 주어진 말을 이용하여 우리말을 영어로 바꿔 쓰세요.

1 그 수업은 2시 30분에 끝났다. (finish)

➡ ___The class finished at 2:30.___

2 많은 사람들이 가을에 캐나다를 방문한다. (many, visit, fall)

➡ _____

3 나는 내 생일에 가족들과 저녁 식사를 했다. (have dinner with)

➡ _____

4 그녀는 그곳에서 5년 동안 일했다. (there)

➡ _____

5 그는 여름휴가 동안 일해야 한다. (have to, the summer holiday)

➡ _____

TIP 1

요일, 날짜 외에도 특정한 날 앞에는 전치사 on을 사용해요.

e.g.
- on Monday
- on July 3
- on New Year's Day
- on Sunday morning
- on the weekend

6 그들은 회의 전에 점심을 먹었다. (have lunch, the meeting)

➡ _____

7 Ann은 방과 후에 도서관에 갔다. (the library)

➡ _____

TIP 2

for와 during은 모두 '~ 동안'을 의미하지만, for 뒤에는 기간을 나타내는 숫자가, during 뒤에는 특정 명사가 와요.

e.g.
- for a day
  for two hours
  for five months
- during vacation
  during the exam
  during the winter

8 우리는 오전 9시부터 오후 4시까지 수업이 있다. (have class)

➡ _____

9 그는 6시까지 나를 기다렸다. (wait for, o'clock)

➡ _____

10 나의 부모님은 2010년 7월 10일에 결혼하셨다. (get married)

➡ _____

WRAP UP

A Grammar 밑줄 친 부분을 바르게 고치세요.

1 My birthday is <u>in</u> January 19. ➡ _____on_____

2 He will go to Canada <u>on</u> July. ➡ _____

3 His daughter was born <u>at</u> 2017. ➡ _____

4 The train arrived <u>on</u> noon. ➡ _____

5 They play tennis <u>in</u> Sunday morning. ➡ _____

6 I slept <u>during</u> eight hours last night. ➡ _____

7 We are open <u>at</u> 9:00 a.m. to 5:00 p.m. ➡ _____

B Writing 주어진 말을 이용하여 우리말을 영어로 바꿔 쓰세요.

1 그는 10시에 퇴근했다. (leave work, o'clock)

➡ _He left work at 10 o'clock._

2 나는 보통 점심 식사 후에 낮잠을 잔다. (take a nap)

➡ _____

3 그는 6년 동안 해외에서 공부했다. (study abroad)

➡ _____

4 나는 설날에 나의 조부모님을 방문했다. (grandparents, New Year's Day)

➡ _____

5 그 버스는 자정까지 운행한다. (the buses, run, midnight)

➡ _____

C　내신 대비　질문을 읽고, 알맞은 답을 고르세요.

1　밑줄 친 부분이 어색한 것은?

① Roses bloom <u>in</u> spring.

② He went to bed <u>in</u> midnight.

③ We have class <u>at</u> eleven o'clock.

④ She was beautiful <u>on</u> her wedding day.

2　빈칸에 들어갈 말이 순서대로 바르게 짝지어진 것은?

> • She doesn't drink coffee _____ night.
>
> • We took a lot of photos _____ our holiday.

① in – on

② at – for

③ on – from

④ at – during

개념 Review

아래 빈칸을 채우면서 개념을 다시 한번 익혀보세요.

❶ 시간의 전치사 at / in / on

☑ 전치사는 명사 앞에서 ❶ _____ 이나 ❷ _____ 등을 나타내주는 말이에요.

☑ at, in, on은 대표적인 시간 전치사로, ❸ _____ 은 구체적인 시각, 특정한 시점,

❹ _____ 은 연도, 월, 계절 등 비교적 긴 시간, ❺ _____ 은 요일, 날짜, 특정한 날 앞에

사용해요.

❷ 기타 시간의 전치사

☑ 시간을 나타내는 전치사에는 before, after, from ~ to..., for, during, until 등도 있어요.

☑ for와 during은 모두 '~ 동안'을 의미하지만, ❻ _____ 뒤에는 숫자로 된 기간이,

❼ _____ 뒤에는 특정 기간을 나타내는 명사가 와요.

02 장소의 전치사

1 in / on / under / next to

in the box

on the chair

under the table

next to the lamp

전치사	의미				
in	~ 안에, ~에	• 건물, 공간, 용기 등의 내부			
		in the bag	가방 안에	**in** his room	그의 방 안에
		• 마을, 도시, 국가 등 비교적 넓은 장소			
		in Seoul	서울에	**in** China	중국에
on	~ 위에	**on** the desk	책상 위에	**on** the wall	벽에
under	~ 아래에	**under** the sofa	소파 아래에	**under** the tree	나무 아래에
next to	~ 옆에	**next to** the door	문 옆에	**next to** the bank	은행 옆에

☑ 전치사 **in, on, under, next to** 등은 장소나 위치를 나타낼 때 사용해요.

PRACTICE 1 알맞은 장소 전치사 넣기

in	on	under	next to

❶ There is some snow _____on_____ the roof.

❷ The socks are _____ the drawer.

❸ The library is _____ the post office.

❹ The ship passed _____ the bridge.

2 기타 장소의 전치사

in front of the door · · · · · **behind** the fence · · · · · **between** two hats · · · · · **across from** the cat

전치사	의미		
in front of	~ 앞에	**in front of** the school	학교 앞에
behind	~ 뒤에	**behind** the curtain	커튼 뒤에
between	~ 사이에	**between** the bank and the bookstore	은행과 서점 사이에
across from	~ 맞은편에	**across from** my house	우리 집 맞은편에

☑ 장소나 위치를 나타내는 전치사에는 **in front of, behind, between, across from** 등도 있어요.

☑ between은 「**between + 복수 명사 (둘 사이를 의미)**」 또는 **between A and B** 형식으로 사용해요.

PRACTICE 2 알맞은 장소 전치사 넣기

❶ 교회는 시장 맞은편에 있다. → The church is __across from__ the market.

❷ 그는 내 뒤에 앉았다. → He sat _____ me.

❸ 그 자전거는 트럭 앞에 있다. → The bicycle is _____ the truck.

❹ 그 강은 두 나라 사이에 있다. → The river is _____ two countries.

A 사진을 보고 빈칸에 알맞은 전치사를 쓰세요.

1 The books are _____in_____ the bag.

2 The plant is _____ the table.

3 The dog is _____ the desk.

4 The dragonfly is _____ the wall.

5 Some people are _____ the car.

6 The table is _____ two chairs.

7 The cat is _____ the flower basket.

8 The dog is _____ the man.

WORDS plant 식물   dragonfly 잠자리   flower basket 꽃바구니

B (   ) 안에서 알맞은 전치사를 고르세요.

1 My dad is cooking (in, on) the kitchen.

2 Jack lived (on, in) Canada two years ago.

3 Susan hung the picture (on, in) the wall.

4 I live in an apartment (in front of, on) the fifth floor.

5 My friend's house is right (next to, between) our house.

6 The broom is (in, behind) the door.

7 There is a bench (in, under) the tree.

8 Let's meet (in front of, on) the school at 12 o'clock.

9 Don't sit (on, in) the desk. Please sit here.

10 Our tent is (in, between) two trees.

11 He found a coin (in front of, on) the ground.

12 There is some water (under, in) the bottle.

13 The café is (in, between) the bank and the theater.

14 There is something (on, in) your cheek.

15 The drugstore is (across from, between) the bank.

 WORDS hang 걸다, 매달다   **fifth** 다섯 번째의   **broom** 빗자루   **bench** 벤치, 긴 의자   **tent** 텐트   **coin** 동전
ground 땅   **bottle** 병   **café** 카페   **theater** 극장   **cheek** 볼, 뺨   **drugstore** 약국

A 우리말과 같은 뜻이 되도록 빈칸에 알맞은 말을 쓰세요.

1 그는 그의 방에서 공부하고 있다.

→ He is studying ____in____ ____his____ ____room____ .

2 사람들이 바다에서 수영하고 있다.

→ People are swimming _____ _____ _____.

3 그는 그 건물 앞에 차를 주차했다.

→ He parked his car _____ _____ _____ the building.

4 그 소년은 문 뒤에 숨었다.

→ The boy hid _____ _____ _____.

5 나는 그 침대 밑에서 내 휴대 전화를 찾았다.

→ I found my cell phone _____ _____ _____.

6 그녀는 그녀의 얼굴에 로션을 발랐다.

→ She put some lotion _____ _____ _____.

7 그들은 서로 맞은편에 앉아 있다.

→ They are sitting _____ _____ each other.

8 나는 Jack과 Cindy 사이에 앉았다.

→ I sat _____ _____ _____ _____.

9 창문 옆에 있는 남자는 누구니?

→ Who is the man _____ _____ _____ _____?

10 그녀는 그녀의 집 뒤편에 작은 정원을 가지고 있다.

→ She has a small garden _____ _____ _____.

B 주어진 말을 이용하여 우리말을 영어로 바꿔 쓰세요.

1 수족관 안에 물고기가 많이 있다. (a lot of, fish, the aquarium)

➡ ___There are a lot of fish in the aquarium.___

2 그의 셔츠 위에 얼룩이 하나 있다. (a stain, shirt)

➡ _____

3 그녀는 그 사과들을 바구니에 담았다. (put, the apples, the basket)

➡ _____

4 Dave는 Jane과 Mina 사이에 앉아 있다. (sit)

➡ _____

5 그 소녀는 나무 옆에 서 있다. (stand, the tree)

➡ _____

6 그 버스는 호텔 앞에 선다. (stop, the hotel)

➡ _____

7 병원은 미용실 맞은편에 있다. (the hospital, the hair salon)

➡ _____

8 그들은 파라솔 아래서 쉬고 있다. (relax, the beach umbrella)

➡ _____

9 나는 내 연필을 책상 뒤에 떨어뜨렸다. (drop, the desk)

➡ _____

10 서점은 우체국 옆에 있다. (the bookstore, the post office)

➡ _____

TIP 1

같은 장소라도 앞에 오는 전치사에 따라 의미가 달라져요.

e.g.

- There is a boat on the lake. (호수 위에)
- There are a lot of fish in the lake. (호수 안에)

TIP 2

between은 '~ 사이에' 라는 의미로 뒤에 복수 명사나 A and B 형태가 와요.

e.g.

- She is between two boys. (두 소년 사이에)
- She is between Tom and Mike. (Tom과 Mike 사이에)

WRAP UP

A　Grammar　밑줄 친 부분을 바르게 고치세요.

1　There is an apple <u>in</u> the plate.　　➡　　on _____

2　I have some money <u>on</u> my pocket.　➡　_____

3　The carpet is <u>in</u> the floor.　　　　➡　_____

4　The printer is <u>next</u> the computer.　➡　_____

5　Who is the man <u>behind of</u> Tom?　　➡　_____

6　The bicycle is <u>in front from</u> the bus.　➡　_____

7　He sat between Paul <u>or</u> Mike.　　　➡　_____

B　Writing　주어진 말을 이용하여 우리말을 영어로 바꿔 쓰세요.

1　그녀는 주방에서 요리 중이다. (the kitchen)

　➡　　She is cooking in the kitchen. _____

2　소파 위에 쿠션 세 개가 있다. (cushion, the sofa)

　➡　_____

3　그는 나무 아래서 책을 읽고 있다. (a book, the tree)

　➡　_____

4　택시 승강장은 버스 정류장 옆에 있다. (the taxi stand, the bus stop)

　➡　_____

5　경찰서는 소방서 맞은편에 있다. (the police station, the fire station)

　➡　_____

C 　내신 대비　질문을 읽고, 알맞은 답을 고르세요.

1 빈칸에 들어갈 전치사가 <u>다른</u> 하나는?

① The doctor is _____ his office.

② He is swimming _____ the river.

③ She put the soup _____ the bowl.

④ There is something _____ your face.

2 빈칸에 들어갈 말이 순서대로 바르게 짝지어진 것은?

> • Our school is _____ Vine Street and Main Street.
>
> • Room 703 is _____ from room 711.

① in – behind

② on – across

③ next – behind

④ between – across

개념 Review

아래 빈칸을 채우면서 개념을 다시 한번 익혀보세요.

❶ 장소의 전치사 in / on / under / next to

☑ 전치사 in, on, under, next to 등은 ❶ _____ 나 ❷ _____ 를 나타낼 때 사용해요.

❷ 기타 장소의 전치사

☑ 장소나 위치를 나타내는 전치사에는 in front of, behind, between, across from 등도 있어요.

☑ between은 「between + ❸ _____ 」 또는 between A and B 형식으로 사용해요.

[01-02] 대화의 빈칸에 알맞은 말을 고르시오.

01

> A When is your birthday?
> B My birthday is _____ September 10.

① at
② in
③ on
④ for

02

> A Where is Brazil?
> B It's _____ South America.

① in
② on
③ across
④ next to

03 빈칸에 들어갈 말이 순서대로 바르게 짝지어진 것은?

> • He didn't go to bed _____ twelve o'clock.
> • She put a flowerpot in _____ of her house.

① at – next
② in – front
③ until – front
④ for – behind

[04-05] 빈칸에 들어갈 말이 <u>다른</u> 하나를 고르시오.

04 ① I have class _____ Monday afternoon.
② He usually goes to bed _____ midnight.
③ The supermarket is closed _____ Sunday.
④ They usually stay home _____ the weekend.

05 ① The flowers are _____ the vase.
② The man is sitting _____ the car.
③ My brother studied _____ England.
④ There are some clothes _____ the floor.

서술형

[06-07] 우리말과 일치하도록 빈칸에 알맞은 말을 쓰시오.

06

> 그녀는 1시부터 2시까지 수업이 있다.

➡ She has class _____ 1 o'clock _____ 2 o'clock.

07

> 우리 학교 맞은편에는 문구점이 있다.

➡ There is a stationery store _____ _____ our school.

[08-09] 빈칸에 들어갈 말로 알맞지 <u>않은</u> 것을 고르시오.

08

> There are a lot of people _____ the shop.

① in

② on

③ in front of

④ across from

09

> Please put the lamp _____ the table.

① under

② next to

③ behind

④ between

[10-11] 밑줄 친 부분이 틀린 것을 고르시오.

10 ① She drinks some tea <u>after</u> lunch.

② The shop opens early <u>in</u> the morning.

③ He always exercises <u>before</u> breakfast.

④ They played badminton <u>during</u> two hours.

11 ① The pots are <u>on</u> the stove.

② There is a mirror <u>in</u> the wall.

③ The sofa is <u>across from</u> the TV.

④ The cat is sleeping <u>next to</u> the bed.

[12-13] 우리말을 영어로 바르게 옮긴 것을 고르시오.

12

> 그 열차는 1시 30분에 떠난다.

① The train leaves in 1:30.

② The train leaves at 1:30.

③ The train leaves on 1:30.

④ The train leaves for 1:30.

13

> 그 교회 뒤에는 큰 나무 한 그루가 있다.

① There is a big tree behind the church.

② There is a big tree behind to the church.

③ There is a big tree behind of the church.

④ There is a big tree behind from the church.

서술형

[14-15] 주어진 말을 이용하여 우리말을 영어로 바꿔 쓰시오.

14

> 그는 축구 시합 중에 그의 다리를 다쳤다.
> (hurt, the soccer game)

➡ _____

15

> 은행은 카페와 빵집 사이에 있다.
> (the bank, the café, the bakery)

➡ _____

접속사

학습목표

1 등위 접속사가 단어와 구를 연결하는 경우와 절을 연결하는 경우를 구분해서 알아봐요.

2 시간을 의미하는 종속 접속사와 조건, 이유를 의미하는 종속 접속사를 구분해서 알아봐요.

UNIT 01 등위 접속사

1 단어/구를 연결하는 경우

cute **and** small

nice **but** expensive

coffee **or** tea

등위 접속사		
and	I love *Mom and Dad*. It is *warm and sunny*.	나는 엄마와 아빠를 사랑한다. 날씨가 따뜻하고 화창하다.
but	The king was *rich but unhappy*. The shoes are *old but comfortable*.	그 왕은 부유했지만 불행했다. 그 신발은 낡았지만 편하다.
or	You can have *coffee or tea*. Is the baby *a boy or a girl*?	당신은 커피나 차를 마실 수 있어요. 그 아기는 남자니 여자니?

☑ 단어와 단어, 구와 구, 절과 절을 대등하게 연결해주는 말을 **등위 접속사**라고 해요.

☑ **and**(~와, 그리고)는 서로 비슷한 내용을, **but**(~지만, 그러나)은 서로 반대되는 내용을 연결할 때 사용해요. **or**(~거나, 또는)는 둘 중 하나를 가리키는 경우에 사용해요.

PRACTICE 1 알맞은 말 넣기

fun	pears	shiny	on foot

❶ Her hair is long and _____shiny_____

❷ The ride was scary but _____.

❸ Do you go to school by bus or _____?

❹ She bought some grapes, mangoes, and _____.

2 절을 연결하는 경우

It rained a lot, **but** I went out.

It rained a lot, **so** I didn't go out.

등위 접속사		
and	*I have a brother, **and** his name is Bill.*	나는 형이 있는데, 이름이 Bill이다.
but	*He borrowed a book, **but** he didn't read it.*	그는 책을 빌렸지만, 읽지는 않았다.
or	*Are you busy, **or** do you have time?*	너는 바쁘니, 아니면 시간이 있니?
so	*I was tired, **so** I went to bed early.*	나는 피곤해서, 일찍 잤다.

☑ 등위 접속사가 절과 절을 연결할 때는 접속사 앞에 **콤마(,)**를 넣어요.

☑ **so**는 '그래서'라는 뜻으로 원인과 결과를 나타내는 절을 연결할 때 사용해요.

PRACTICE 2 문장 연결하기

❶ I arrived at home, and •　　　　• he bought a new one.

❷ I had a cold, so •　　　　• I had dinner.

❸ He has a cell phone, but •　　　　• do you want to go?

❹ Will you wait for me, or •　　　　• I took some medicine.

 문법 쏙쏙

A (   ) 안에서 알맞은 접속사를 고르세요.

1 I have one brother (and, or, but) two sisters.

2 The weather was sunny (and, or, but) cold.

3 Was the concert good (and, or, but) bad?

4 We had a pizza (and, or, but) pasta for dinner.

5 Would you like chicken (and, or, but) beef?

6 Jack is wearing a T-shirt (and, or, but) shorts.

7 Fast food is delicious (and, or, but) unhealthy.

8 Is your sister younger (and, or, but) older than you?

9 The flag is white, black, red, (and, or, but) blue.

10 Would you like to pay with cash (and, or, but) by credit card?

11 They were tired (and, or, so) hungry after the game.

12 It was hot, (but, or, so) we went swimming.

13 I like singing, (but, or, so) I'm not good at it.

14 You can take bus number 8 (but, or, so) 9.

15 I watched the film, (but, or, so) I didn't enjoy it.

 WORDS concert 연주회, 콘서트   beef 쇠고기   shorts 반바지   unhealthy 건강하지 못한; 건강에 해로운   flag 기, 깃발
cash 현금   credit card 신용카드   be good at ~을 잘하다   film 영화 (= movie)

B and, or, but, so를 이용하여 두 문장을 한 문장으로 바꿔 쓰세요.

1 I am 14 years old. My sister is 12 years old.

➡ ___I am 14 years old, and my sister is 12 years old.___

2 It is a great house. It doesn't have a yard.

➡ _____

3 We can eat out. We can eat at home.

➡ _____

4 It was cold. I turned on the heater.

➡ _____

5 My little brother can read. He can't write.

➡ _____

6 The bus stopped. A woman got off.

➡ _____

7 The movie was boring. I fell asleep.

➡ _____

8 Tom gave his girlfriend a present. She loved it.

➡ _____

9 You can fix your bike. You can buy a new one.

➡ _____

10 You can walk to the station. It's a little far.

➡ _____

WORDS yard 마당, 뜰 eat out 외식하다 turn on ~을 켜다 heater 난방기, 히터 get off 내리다, 하차하다
fall asleep 잠들다 present 선물 fix 고치다 a little 조금, 약간 far (거리가) 먼

영작 술술

A 우리말과 같은 뜻이 되도록 빈칸에 알맞은 말을 쓰세요.

1 초록색과 노란색은 내가 가장 좋아하는 색이다.

→ Green ____and____ yellow are my favorite colors.

2 그 책은 지루했지만 유용했다.

→ The book was boring _____ useful.

3 너는 청소를 할 거니 요리를 할 거니?

→ Will you clean _____ cook?

4 우리는 시장에 가서 약간의 음식을 샀다.

→ We went to the market _____ bought some food.

5 그녀는 추워서 코트를 입었다.

→ She was cold, _____ she put on her coat.

6 나는 노래는 할 수 있지만, 춤은 출 수 없다.

→ I can sing, _____ I _____ _____.

7 너는 TV 보는 것을 원하니 음악 듣는 것을 원하니?

→ Do you want to watch TV _____ _____ to music?

8 그는 기타를 연주하고, 나는 키보드를 연주했다.

→ He played the guitar, _____ I _____ the keyboard.

9 Tom은 손은 씻었지만, 세수는 하지 않았다.

→ Tom washed his hands, _____ he _____ _____ his face.

10 나는 일해야 해서, Sam의 파티에 갈 수 없다.

→ I have to work, _____ I _____ _____ to Sam's party.

B 주어진 말을 이용하여 우리말을 영어로 바꿔 쓰세요.

1 그 방은 깨끗하고 잘 정돈되어 있다. (the room, tidy)

→   The room is clean and tidy.

2 그 답은 맞니 틀리니? (the answer, right, wrong)

→

3 그녀는 똑똑하지만 건망증이 있다. (smart, forgetful)

→

4 그녀는 집에 가서 휴식을 취했다. (get some rest)

→

5 나는 그의 얼굴은 알지만, 나는 그의 이름은 모른다. (know)

→

6 우리는 공원에 가거나, 집에 머무를 수 있다. (stay at home)

→

7 어두워서, 나는 불을 켰다. (it, turn on the light)

→

8 그 음식은 맛있었고, 서비스도 훌륭했다. (delicious, excellent)

→

9 그는 돈이 좀 필요해서, 아르바이트를 구했다. (get a part-time job)

→

10 나는 외출하고 싶었지만, 비가 내리기 시작했다. (want to, start raining)

→

TIP 1

등위 접속사로 연결되는 부분은 서로 대등한 관계이어야 해요.

e.g.
- I like apples and bananas. (명사＋명사)
- It was sunny but cold. (형용사＋형용사)
- Fish cannot walk or fly. (동사＋동사)

TIP 2

등위 접속사가 절과 절을 연결할 때는 접속사 앞에 콤마(,)를 넣어요.

e.g.
- It was hot, so I went swimming.

WRAP UP

A Grammar 밑줄 친 부분을 바르게 고치세요.

1 Would you like soup <u>and</u> salad? ➡ _____ or _____

2 She is wearing earrings <u>but</u> a necklace. ➡ _____

3 They tried really hard <u>or</u> lost the game. ➡ _____

4 We can go by bus, <u>so</u> we can walk. ➡ _____

5 She read a book, <u>but</u> she liked it. ➡ _____

6 I don't have any money, <u>but</u> I can't go shopping. ➡ _____

7 Tom likes playing soccer, <u>so</u> he isn't good at it. ➡ _____

B Writing 주어진 말을 이용하여 우리말을 영어로 바꿔 쓰세요.

1 곰과 뱀은 위험한 동물이다. (bears, snakes, dangerous)

➡ Bears and snakes are dangerous animals.

2 그는 New York이나 L.A.로 이사 갈 것이다. (will, move to)

➡ _____

3 그녀는 생선은 먹지만, 고기는 먹지 않는다. (eat, fish, meat)

➡ _____

4 비가 많이 와서, 우리는 나가지 않았다. (a lot, go out)

➡ _____

5 나는 스페인 친구가 있는데, 그녀의 이름은 Luisa이다. (a Spanish friend)

➡ _____

C 내신 대비 질문을 읽고, 알맞은 답을 고르세요.

1 밑줄 친 부분이 어색한 것은?

① I called Mike, <u>but</u> he didn't answer.

② We stayed at home <u>and</u> watched TV.

③ She wants to be a doctor <u>or</u> a teacher.

④ It was his birthday, <u>so</u> he didn't invite me.

2 빈칸에 들어갈 말이 순서대로 바르게 짝지어진 것은?

> • Whales live in the sea, _____ they are not fish.
>
> • I have an exam tomorrow, _____ I have to study tonight.

① so – or

② but – so

③ but – or

④ and – but

개념 Review

아래 빈칸을 채우면서 개념을 다시 한번 익혀보세요.

❶ 등위 접속사: 단어 / 구를 연결하는 경우

☑ 단어와 단어, 구와 구, 절과 절을 대등하게 연결해주는 말을 ❶_____ 라고 해요.

☑ ❷_____ (~와, 그리고)는 서로 비슷한 내용을, ❸_____ (~지만, 그러나)은 서로 반대되는
내용을 연결할 때 사용해요. ❹_____ (~거나, 또는)는 둘 중 하나를 가리키는 경우에 사용해요.

❷ 등위 접속사: 절을 연결하는 경우

☑ 등위 접속사가 절과 절을 연결할 때는 접속사 앞에 ❺_____ 를 넣어요.

☑ ❻_____ 는 '그래서'라는 뜻으로 원인과 결과를 나타내는 절을 연결할 때 사용해요.

UNIT 02 종속 접속사

1 when / before / after

I listen to music **when I'm on the train.**

I finished studying **before Mom got home.**

종속 접속사		
when	I feel happy **when I am with you.** **When he was a child,** he lived in France.	나는 너와 함께 있을 때 행복하다. 그는 어렸을 때, 프랑스에 살았다.
before	The bus left **before we arrived.** I brush my teeth **before I go to bed.**	그 버스는 우리가 도착하기 전에 떠났다. 나는 자기 전에 이를 닦는다.
after	Ann dried her hair **after she washed it.** It got cold **after the rain stopped.**	Ann은 머리를 감은 후 말렸다. 비가 그친 후 추워졌다.

☑ **when**은 '~할 때', **before**는 '~ 전에', **after**는 '~ 후에'라는 의미의 **종속 접속사**로, 종속 접속사가 이끄는 절은 단독으로 쓰일 수 없어요.

☑ 종속 접속사가 이끄는 절이 문장 앞에 오면 절과 절 사이에 **콤마(,)**를 넣어요.

e.g. **Before we arrived,** the bus left.

PRACTICE 1 문장 연결하기

❶ He was so shy • • before he left home.

❷ We went for a walk • • after we had dinner.

❸ She was 27 years old • • when I first met him.

❹ He turned off all the lights • • when she got married.

2 if /because

If you eat fast food, you will gain weight.

I turned on the fan **because it was hot.**

종속 접속사		
if	You can stay here **if you want.** **If we don't hurry,** we will be late.	네가 원한다면 여기 머물러도 돼. 우리는 서두르지 않는다면, 늦을 것이다.
because	He was late **because traffic was bad.** I drank some water **because I was thirsty.**	교통 상황이 나빴기 때문에 그는 늦었다. 나는 목이 말랐기 때문에 물을 마셨다.

☑ **if**는 '(만약) ~하다면'의 의미로 조건을 나타낼 때 사용해요. if가 이끄는 절에서는 미래 시제 대신 **현재 시제**를 사용해요.
   e.g. We will be late **if** we will not hurry. **(X)**

☑ **because**는 '~ 때문에'의 의미로 원인이나 이유를 나타낼 때 사용해요.

PRACTICE 2 **if /because 넣기**

❶ I like babies ___because___ they are so cute.

❷ _____ you feel hungry, you can eat the food.

❸ She opened the windows _____ it was too hot.

❹ You will miss the bus _____ you walk too slowly.

문법 쏙쏙

[보기]에서 가장 알맞은 말을 골라 문장을 완성하세요.

when I grow up	if you turn left
after he woke up	before she went to Paris
because it is a holiday	after he ran the marathon
if you don't have a map	because he hurt his leg
before the movie started	when the alarm clock rang

1 I woke up _____ when the alarm clock rang _____.

2 She studied French _____.

3 He opened the curtains _____.

4 You will see the building _____.

5 The shops are closed _____.

6 We bought some popcorn _____.

7 I want to be a doctor _____.

8 He was tired _____.

9 You will get lost _____.

10 He stayed at home _____.

WORDS grow up 성장하다, 자라다　wake up (잠에서) 깨다　holiday 휴일　turn left 좌측으로 돌다
marathon 마라톤　alarm clock 자명종　French 프랑스어　get lost 길을 잃다

B 주어진 접속사를 이용하여 두 문장을 한 문장으로 바꿔 쓰세요.

1 I turned on the air conditioner. It was hot. (because)

→   I turned on the air conditioner because it was hot.

2 I drink too much coffee. I can't sleep at night. (if)

→   If I drink too much coffee, I can't sleep at night.

3 I must go to the bank. It closes. (before)

→ _____

4 She went out. She locked the door. (when)

→ _____

5 Jean hung out the clothes to dry. She washed them. (after)

→ _____

6 It snows. I will make a snowman. (if)

→ _____

7 I always wash my hands. I eat food. (before)

→ _____

8 I don't like big cities. They are too crowded. (because)

→ _____

9 I will buy the car. The price goes down. (if)

→ _____

10 I was a child. I didn't eat spinach. (when)

→ _____

WORDS   **air conditioner** 에어컨   **lock** 잠그다   **hang out** (빨래를) 널다   **snowman** 눈사람
crowded 붐비는, 복잡한   **price** 가격   **go down** (가격·기온 등이) 내려가다   **spinach** 시금치

A 우리말과 같은 뜻이 되도록 빈칸에 알맞은 말을 쓰세요.

1 날씨가 더울 때, 나는 물을 많이 마신다.

→ __When__ the weather __is__ __hot__ , I drink a lot of water.

2 그는 길을 건너기 전에 좌우를 살폈다.

→ He looked both ways _____ he _____ the street.

3 너는 규칙적으로 운동한다면, 더 건강해질 것이다.

→ _____ you _____ regularly, you will be healthier.

4 그녀는 숙제를 끝마친 후 자러 갔다.

→ She went to bed _____ she _____ her homework.

5 그는 아팠기 때문에 학교에 오지 않았다.

→ He didn't come to school _____ he _____ _____ .

6 나는 집을 나서기 전에 우산을 챙겼다.

→ I took my umbrella _____ I _____ home.

7 그는 햄버거 두 개를 먹었기 때문에 배가 불렀다.

→ He was full _____ he _____ two hamburgers.

8 내가 곤경에 빠졌을 때, 그가 나를 도와주었다.

→ _____ I _____ in trouble, he helped me.

9 그녀는 이를 닦은 후에, 간식을 먹지 않는다.

→ _____ she _____ _____ _____ , she doesn't eat any snacks.

10 네가 늦게 일어난다면, 학교에 지각할 것이다.

→ _____ you _____ _____ late, you will be late for school.

B 주어진 말을 이용하여 우리말을 영어로 바꿔 쓰세요.

1 나는 집에 있을 때, 보통 TV를 본다. (usually)

→ When I am home, I usually watch TV.

2 그는 떠나기 전에 꽃에 물을 주었다. (water, the flowers, leave)

→ _____

3 나는 열심히 공부했기 때문에 그 시험에 합격했다. (pass the exam)

→ _____

4 당신은 서두르지 않는다면, 그 버스를 놓칠 것이다. (hurry, miss)

→ _____

5 그는 샤워를 하고 난 후 상쾌함을 느꼈다. (refreshed, take a shower)

→ _____

6 그녀는 나를 봤을 때, 나에게 손을 흔들었다. (wave at)

→ _____

7 그는 도쿄에 가기 전에 호텔 객실을 예약했다.

(book a hotel room, Tokyo)

→ _____

8 나는 그 가수를 좋아했기 때문에 그 콘서트에 갔다. (the singer)

→ _____

9 우리가 지하철을 탄다면, 그곳에 더 빨리 도착할 것이다.

(take the subway, get there)

→ _____

10 그는 그 재미있는 농담을 들었을 때 웃었다. (laugh, the funny joke)

→ _____

TIP 1

종속 접속사가 이끄는 절이 문장 앞에 오면 절과 절 사이에 콤마(,)를 넣어요.

e.g.
- It got cold after the rain stopped.
  → After the rain stopped, it got cold.

TIP 2

조건을 뜻하는 접속사 if가 이끄는 절에는 미래 시제를 쓰지 않기 때문에 현재 시제로 대신해요.

e.g.
- If it will rain, I won't go out. (×)
- If it rains, I won't go out. (○)

WRAP UP

A Grammar 서로 알맞은 것끼리 연결하여 문장을 완성하세요.

1 He took off his coat _____d_____   a. if you eat too many sweets.

2 You will get fat _____   b. before we eat.

3 No one was there _____   c. if you don't have a passport.

4 I have to go home _____   d. because it was hot.

5 She went to college _____   e. when I got home.

6 We always pray _____   f. before it's too late.

7 You can't travel abroad _____   g. after she finished high school.

B Writing 주어진 말을 이용하여 우리말을 영어로 바꿔 쓰세요.

1 그녀는 책상에 앉은 후, 교과서를 폈다. (at the desk, her textbook)

→ _After she sat at the desk, she opened her textbook._

2 나는 뉴욕에 있을 때 Jane을 만났다. (in New York)

→ _____

3 그 수업이 지루했기 때문에, 나는 잠이 들었다. (the class, boring, fall asleep)

→ _____

4 나는 나의 부모님이 집에 오시기 전에 집을 청소했다. (the house)

→ _____

5 너는 매일 운동한다면, 살이 빠질 것이다. (exercise, lose weight)

→ _____

C 내신 대비 질문을 읽고, 알맞은 답을 고르세요.

1 두 문장을 한 문장으로 만들 때 빈칸에 들어갈 말로 알맞은 것은?

> Everyone likes him. He is kind.
>
> → Everyone likes him _____ he is kind.

① if   ② after

③ when   ④ because

2 우리말을 영어로 옮길 때 빈칸에 들어갈 말이 바르게 짝지어진 것은?

> 내일 비가 오면, 우리는 소풍을 취소할 것이다.
>
> → If it _____ tomorrow, we _____ the picnic.

① rains – cancel   ② will rain – cancel

③ rains – will cancel   ④ will rain – will cancel

개념 Review

아래 빈칸을 채우면서 개념을 다시 한번 익혀보세요.

❶ 종속 접속사: when / before / after

☑ **❶** _____ 은 '~할 때', **❷** _____ 는 '~ 전에', **❸** _____ 는 '~ 후에'라는 의미의 종속 접속사로, 종속 접속사가 이끄는 절은 단독으로 쓰일 수 없어요.

☑ 종속 접속사가 이끄는 절이 문장 앞에 오면 절과 절 사이에 **❹** _____ 를 넣어요.

❷ 종속 접속사: if / because

☑ if는 '(만약) ~하다면'의 의미로 조건을 나타낼 때 사용해요. if가 이끄는 절에서는 미래 시제 대신 **❺** _____ 를 사용해요.

☑ because는 '~ 때문에'의 의미로 원인이나 이유를 나타낼 때 사용해요.

[01-02] 대화의 빈칸에 알맞은 말을 고르시오.

01

> A Do you live in a house _____
>   an apartment?
> B I live in a house.

① and

② but

③ or

④ so

02

> A What did you do yesterday?
> B I stayed at home _____
>   I didn't feel well.

① if

② when

③ before

④ because

[03-04] 빈칸에 들어갈 말로 알맞은 것을 고르시오.

03

> Bill has a guitar, _____ he plays
> it really well.

① and

② but

③ when

④ because

04

> Jane gave me some cookies
> _____ she baked them.

① so

② and

③ after

④ before

05 빈칸에 들어갈 말이 순서대로 바르게 짝지어진 것은?

> • I can help you, _____ you
>   don't have to worry.
> • She drank a glass of milk
>   _____ she went to bed.

① so – if

② or – when

③ so – before

④ but – because

서술형

[06-07] 우리말과 같은 뜻이 되도록 빈칸에 알맞은 말을 쓰시오.

06

> 너는 더 조심해서 운전하지 않으면, 사고를 당할 것이다.

→ _____ you _____
_____ more carefully, you will
have an accident.

07

> 나는 캐나다에 있었을 때 그 사진을 찍었다.

→ I took the picture _____
I _____ in Canada.

[08-09] 밑줄 친 부분이 **틀린** 것을 고르시오.

08 ① Is that book interesting <u>or</u> boring?

② He got on the bus <u>and</u> took a seat.

③ I visited him, <u>so</u> he was out of town.

④ She is not pretty <u>but</u> is so popular.

09 ① The phone rang <u>when</u> we had dinner.

② She felt better <u>after</u> she got some rest.

③ The store was closed <u>because</u> it was very late.

④ <u>Before</u> you walk faster, you will catch the train.

10 다음 중 **틀린** 문장은?

① I will call you if I will be too late.

② She plays the piano when she feels lonely.

③ She made a list before she went to the market.

④ I wanted to eat pizza, so I went to an Italian restaurant.

11 빈칸에 들어갈 접속사가 **다른** 하나는?

① Our teacher is strict _____ generous.

② She is Korean, _____ she lives in Japan.

③ He has a car, _____ he wants a new one.

④ He went to the bathroom _____ took a shower.

[12-13] 우리말을 영어로 바르게 옮긴 것을 고르시오.

12

그의 펜이 없어져서, 그는 나의 것을 사용했다.

① His pen was lost, or he used mine.

② His pen was lost, so he used mine.

③ His pen was lost, but he used mine.

④ His pen was lost because he used mine.

13

나는 연극이 끝나기 전에 나갔다.

① I went out before the play ended.

② Before I went out, the play ended.

③ When I went out, the play ended.

④ I went out after the play ended.

서술형

[14-15] 주어진 말을 이용하여 우리말을 영어로 바꿔 쓰시오.

14

그는 부유하지만, 많은 돈을 쓰지는 않는다.
(rich, spend much money)

➡ _____

15

너는 지금 먹지 않는다면, 나중에 배가 고플 것이다. (later)

➡ _____

06

감탄문과 명령문

학습목표

1   What으로 시작하는 감탄문과 How로 시작하는 감탄문의 형태와 의미를 알아봐요.

2   긍정 명령문과 부정 명령문의 형태와 의미를 알아봐요.

UNIT 01 감탄문

1 What으로 시작하는 감탄문

What a pretty dress it is!

What colorful balloons she has!

감탄문 형식		
What(+a/an)+형용사+ 명사+주어+동사!	What a cute girl she is! What a bright smile he has! What nice shoes they are! What lovely weather it is!	그녀는 참 귀여운 소녀구나! 그는 참 밝은 미소를 가졌구나! 그건 참 멋진 신발이구나! 참 좋은 날씨구나!

☑ 감탄문은 '참 ~하구나!'라는 의미로 기쁨, 놀라움, 슬픔 등의 감정을 나타내는 문장이에요.

☑ What으로 시작하는 감탄문은 「What(+a/an)+형용사+명사+주어+동사!」의 어순이에요. 이때 마지막의 「주어+동사」는 생략할 수 있어요.

PRACTICE 1 감탄문 만들기

❶ He is a very rude man. ➡ ___What a rude man he is!___

❷ They are very kind people. ➡ _____

❸ She has very beautiful eyes. ➡ _____

❹ I made a very stupid mistake. ➡ _____

2 How로 시작하는 감탄문

How cute my dog is!

How happily they sing!

감탄문 형식		
How + 형용사/부사 + 주어 + 동사!	**How kind** you are! **How boring** this movie is! **How fast** he runs! **How brilliantly** the stars shine!	너는 참 친절하구나! 이 영화는 참 지루하구나! 그는 참 빨리 달리는구나! 별들이 참 환하게 빛나는구나!

☑ How로 시작하는 감탄문은 「How + 형용사/부사 + 주어 + 동사!」의 어순이에요. 이때 마지막의 「주어 + 동사」는 생략할 수 있어요.

PRACTICE 2   감탄문 만들기

❶ The boy is eating very slowly.   →   How slowly the boy is eating!

❷ This shopping bag is very heavy.   →   _____

❸ She paints very beautifully.   →   _____

❹ You play the guitar very well.   →   _____

A ( ) 안에서 알맞은 말을 고르세요.

1 (What, How) delicious this cake is!

2 (What, How) a funny joke it is!

3 (What, How) beautiful the woman is!

4 (What, How) a pretty garden she has!

5 (What, How) well you speak English!

6 (What, How) a big truck he drives!

7 (What, How) generous the man is!

8 (What, How) easy the exam was!

9 (What, How) lovely children she has!

10 (What, How) expensive these shoes are!

11 (What, How) high oil prices are!

12 (What, How) a good family you have!

13 (What, How) slow this computer is!

14 (What, How) beautiful weather it is!

15 (What, How) an interesting idea it is!

WORDS joke 농담   truck 트럭, 화물차   generous 너그러운   lovely 사랑스러운, 예쁜   oil price 유가, 석유 가격

B 주어진 문장을 What 또는 How로 시작하는 감탄문으로 바꿔 쓰세요.

1 It is a very high mountain.

➡ What a high mountain it is!

2 Your daughter is very clever.

➡ How clever your daughter is!

3 He is a very good cook.

➡ _____

4 These jeans are very cheap.

➡ _____

5 I am very tired.

➡ _____

6 She has very long legs.

➡ _____

7 He dances very badly.

➡ _____

8 I made a very big mistake.

➡ _____

9 The rabbit ran away very quickly.

➡ _____

10 You are wearing a very nice jacket.

➡ _____

WORDS   daughter 딸   clever 영리한   cook 요리사; 요리하다   jeans 청바지   cheap (값이) 싼   leg 다리
badly 서투르게; 나쁘게   make a mistake 실수하다   rabbit 토끼   run away 달아나다, 도망치다

A 우리말과 같은 뜻이 되도록 빈칸에 알맞은 말을 쓰세요.

1 그는 참 게으른 소년이구나!

➡ ___What___ ___a___ lazy boy he is!

2 노을이 참 아름답구나!

➡ _____ beautiful the sunset is!

3 그건 참 지저분한 방이구나!

➡ _____ _____ messy room it is!

4 그녀는 참 매력적이구나!

➡ _____ attractive she is!

5 그건 참 오래된 집이구나!

➡ _____ _____ old house it is!

6 우리는 참 멋진 시간을 보냈구나!

➡ _____ a great time we had!

7 너는 오늘 참 멋져 보이는구나!

➡ _____ wonderful you look today!

8 그는 춤을 참 잘 추는구나!

➡ _____ well he dances!

9 그녀는 참 큰 눈을 가졌구나!

➡ _____ big eyes she has!

10 이 쿠키들은 참 맛있구나!

➡ _____ tasty these cookies are!

B 주어진 말을 이용하여 우리말을 영어로 바꿔 쓰세요.

1 너는 참 큰 집을 갖고 있구나! (what, a big house)

➡ ___What a big house you have!___

2 너는 참 좋은 친구구나! (what, a good friend)

➡ _____

3 그 시계는 참 비싸구나! (how, the watch)

➡ _____

4 그것은 참 아름다운 산이구나! (what, a beautiful mountain)

➡ _____

5 이 아이들은 참 귀엽구나! (how, these children)

➡ _____

6 나는 참 운이 좋구나! (how, lucky)

➡ _____

7 그녀는 프랑스어를 참 잘하는구나! (how, speak French)

➡ _____

8 그 이야기는 참 놀랍구나! (how, amazing, the story)

➡ _____

9 너는 참 훌륭한 일을 했구나! (what, a great job)

➡ _____

10 이 수학 연습문제들은 참 어렵구나! (how, these math exercises)

➡ _____

TIP 1

What으로 시작하는 감탄문의 어순은 「What (+a/an)+형용사+명사 +주어+동사!」이며, 이때 「주어+동사」는 생략할 수 있어요.

e.g.
- She is a very cute girl.
  → What a cute girl she is!
- It is very nice weather.
  → What nice weather it is!

TIP 2

How로 시작하는 감탄문의 어순은 「How+형용사/ 부사+주어+동사!」이며, 이때 「주어+동사」는 생략할 수 있어요.

e.g.
- She is very cute.
  → How cute she is!
- The weather is very nice.
  → How nice the weather is!

WRAP UP

A Grammar 밑줄 친 부분을 바르게 고쳐 문장을 다시 쓰세요.

1 How a nice picture it is! → What a nice picture it is!

2 How busy is the street! → _____

3 What tall a building it is! → _____

4 How the swan beautiful is! → _____

5 What beautifully she sings! → _____

6 What a lovely weather it is! → _____

7 How brave boys they are! → _____

B Writing 주어진 말을 이용하여 우리말을 영어로 바꿔 쓰세요.

1 그는 참 수줍음이 많구나! (how, shy)

→ How shy he is!

2 그건 참 멋진 풍경이구나! (what, a great landscape)

→ _____

3 너는 참 멋진 모자를 가졌구나! (what, a nice hat)

→ _____

4 이 셔츠들은 참 작구나! (how, these shirts)

→ _____

5 그녀는 일을 참 빨리 하는구나! (how, fast)

→ _____

C 【내신 대비】 질문을 읽고, 알맞은 답을 고르세요.

1 다음 중 <u>틀린</u> 문장은?

① How thick the book is!

② What a sad ending it is!

③ How surprising news it is!

④ What cute puppies they are!

2 우리말을 영어로 옮길 때 빈칸에 들어갈 말로 알맞은 것은?

> 이것은 참 비싼 차구나!
>
> → _____ this is!

① How expensive car

② What expensive a car

③ How an expensive car

④ What an expensive car

개념 Review

아래 빈칸을 채우면서 개념을 다시 한번 익혀보세요.

❶ What으로 시작하는 감탄문

☑ 감탄문은 '참 ~하구나!'라는 의미로 기쁨, 놀라움, 슬픔 등의 ❶ _____ 을 나타내는 문장이에요.

☑ What으로 시작하는 감탄문은 「What(+a/an)+ ❷ _____ + ❸ _____ +주어+동사!」의 어순이에요. 이때 마지막의 「주어+동사」는 생략할 수 있어요.

❷ How로 시작하는 감탄문

☑ How로 시작하는 감탄문은 「How+ ❹ _____ +주어+동사!」의 어순이에요. 이때 마지막의 「주어+동사」는 생략할 수 있어요.

UNIT 02 명령문

1 긍정 명령문

Stop using your phone.

Be quiet, please.

긍정 명령문 형식		
동사원형 ~	Open your book. Move this chair.	책을 펴라. 이 의자를 옮겨라.
동사원형 ~, please	Please sit down. Close the window, please.	앉아주세요. 창문을 닫아주세요.

☑ **명령문**(~해라)은 상대방에게 무엇을 시키거나 어떤 행동을 하도록 요구하는 문장으로, **동사원형**으로 시작해요.

☑ 명령문 앞이나 뒤에 **please**를 붙이면 보다 공손한 표현이 돼요.

PRACTICE 1 긍정 명령문 만들기

Answer	Be	Walk	Wash

❶ ___Answer___ the phone, please.

❷ _____ careful!

❸ _____ your hands before you eat.

❹ _____ slowly, please.

2 부정 명령문

Don't smoke in this building.

Don't be late for school.

부정 명령문 형식

Don't + 동사원형 ~	Don't turn up the volume.	볼륨을 높이지 마.
	Don't make any noise.	떠들지 마.
	Don't be noisy in the library.	도서관에서 떠들지 마.
	Don't leave now.	지금 떠나지 마.

☑ **부정 명령문**은 '~하지 마라'라는 의미로 긍정 명령문 앞에 **Don't**를 붙여서 만들어요.

PRACTICE 2 부정 명령문 만들기

eat   be   play   forget

① ___Don't___ ___play___ the music too loudly.

② _____ _____ your homework.

③ _____ _____ rude to your teacher.

④ _____ _____ too much junk food.

문법 쏙쏙

A [보기]에서 알맞은 말을 골라 명령문을 완성하세요.

be	fight	have	help
hurry	move	open	put on
stop	turn down	wash	yell

1 ____Open____ the window, please. It's hot in here.

2 _____ up! We are late!

3 Don't _____ afraid. I'll help you.

4 _____ talking and listen to me.

5 _____ the volume, please.

6 Please _____ the table to the corner.

7 _____ your coat. It's cold outside.

8 Go and _____ your hands.

9 Don't _____ with your brother.

10 Always _____ poor people.

11 _____ some cake. It's delicious.

12 Don't _____ at people. It's very rude.

✏️ **WORDS** fight 싸우다 put on ~을 입다 turn down (소리·온도 등을) 낮추다 yell 소리 지르다 rude 무례한

B 주어진 동사를 이용하여 명령문을 완성하세요. (필요시 Don't를 넣을 것)

1 _____Wash_____ the dishes, please. (wash)

2 _____ the artwork. (touch)

3 _____ nice to people. (be)

4 _____ some water. You look thirsty. (drink)

5 _____ a mess. I just cleaned the room. (make)

6 _____! I can't swim. (help)

7 _____ a good time on your holiday. (have)

8 I'm not ready yet. Please _____ for me. (wait)

9 _____ there. Sit down, please. (stand)

10 _____ your textbook to page 70, please. (open)

11 _____ here and look out the window. (come)

12 _____ your alarm clock and get up early. (set)

13 _____ careful. The roads are icy. (be)

14 _____ to lock the door. (forget)

15 Please _____. Stay here with me. (go)

WORDS artwork 미술품   thirsty 목마른   make a mess 어지럽히다   textbook 교과서
set an alarm clock 자명종을 맞추다   icy 얼음에 뒤덮인

영작 술술

A 우리말과 같은 뜻이 되도록 빈칸에 알맞은 말을 쓰세요.

1 네 방을 청소해라.

  → ___Clean___ your room.

2 내 숙제를 도와줘.

  → _____ me with my homework.

3 밤에는 피아노를 치지 마.

  → _____ _____ the piano at night.

4 잘 듣고 질문에 답하세요.

  → _____ carefully and _____ the question.

5 내 물건을 만지지 마.

  → _____ _____ my things.

6 의자에 앉으세요.

  → Please _____ on the chair.

7 커피를 너무 많이 마시지 마.

  → _____ _____ too much coffee.

8 차를 운전할 때에는 조심해.

  → _____ careful when you drive a car.

9 박물관 안에서는 사진을 찍지 마세요.

  → _____ _____ photos in the museum.

10 다시는 늦지 마. 알겠니?

  → _____ _____ late again. Okay?

B 주어진 말을 이용하여 우리말을 영어로 바꿔 쓰세요.

1 에너지를 절약해라. (energy)

➡ <u>Save energy.</u>

2 그 버튼을 누르지 마. (press, the button)

➡ _____

3 당신의 안전벨트를 매세요. (wear, seatbelt, please)

➡ _____

4 네 장난감들을 치워라. (put away)

➡ _____

5 그것에 대해 걱정하지 마. (worry about it)

➡ _____

6 네 휴대 전화를 꺼라. (turn off, cell phone)

➡ _____

7 그의 충고를 따르지 마. (follow, advice)

➡ _____

8 실내에서는 네 신발을 벗어라. (take off, indoors)

➡ _____

9 도서관 앞에서 소리 지르지 마세요. (shout, in front of)

➡ _____

10 시끄럽게 하지 마세요. (make any noise)

➡ _____

WRAP UP

A Grammar 밑줄 친 부분을 바르게 고쳐 문장을 다시 쓰세요.

1 <u>Do have</u> some food. → ___Have some food.___

2 <u>Not eat</u> too many sweets. → _____

3 <u>Helping</u> yourself. → _____

4 Don't <u>making</u> a mess. → _____

5 <u>Do</u> careful. → _____

6 <u>Does</u> your homework. → _____

7 <u>Leave not</u> the door open. → _____

B Writing 주어진 말을 이용하여 우리말을 영어로 바꿔 쓰세요.

1 이곳에 서명해주세요. (sign, please)

→ ___Sign here, please.[Please sign here.]___

2 가서 재미있게 놀아. (have fun)

→ _____

3 저녁 먹기 전에 네 손을 씻어. (before dinner)

→ _____

4 탄산음료를 너무 많이 마시지 마. (too much soda)

→ _____

5 네 우산을 잊지 마. (forget)

→ _____

C 내신 대비 질문을 읽고, 알맞은 답을 고르세요.

1 다음 중 <u>틀린</u> 문장은?

① Don't say anything about it.

② Don't turning on the heater.

③ Bring your sister to the party.

④ Have some cookies if you want.

2 우리말을 영어로 옮길 때 빈칸에 들어갈 말로 알맞은 것은?

> 실수하는 것을 두려워하지 마.
>
> → _____ afraid of making mistakes.

① Don't

② Be not

③ Don't be

④ Don't you be

개념 Review

아래 빈칸을 채우면서 개념을 다시 한번 익혀보세요.

1 긍정 명령문

☑ 명령문(~해라)은 상대방에게 무엇을 시키거나 어떤 행동을 하도록 요구하는 문장으로, ❶ _____ 으로 시작해요.

☑ 명령문 앞이나 뒤에 ❷ _____ 를 붙이면 보다 공손한 표현이 돼요.

2 부정 명령문

☑ 부정 명령문은 '~하지 마라'라는 의미로 긍정 명령문 앞에 ❸ _____ 를 붙여서 만들어요.

[01-02] 대화의 빈칸에 알맞은 말을 고르시오.

01

> A _____ beautiful day it is!
> B Yeah, let's go on a picnic!

① How
② What
③ How a
④ What a

02

> A Please _____ touch the door. The paint is still wet.
> B Okay. I will be careful.

① do
② not
③ isn't
④ don't

[03-04] 다음 문장을 감탄문으로 바꿀 때, 빈칸에 들어갈 말로 알맞은 것을 고르시오.

03

> He has a very nice car.
> → _____ car he has!

① How nice
② What nice
③ How a nice
④ What a nice

04

> She will be very happy.
> → _____ she will be!

① How happy
② What happy
③ How a happy
④ What a happy

05 빈칸에 들어갈 말이 순서대로 바르게 짝지어진 것은?

> • _____ kind people they are!
> • _____ quiet in the library.

① How – Do
② What – Be
③ How – Don't
④ What – Please

서술형

[06-07] 우리말과 같은 뜻이 되도록 주어진 말을 바르게 배열하시오.

06

> 그것은 참 재미있는 영화구나!
> (an, movie, interesting, what, is, it)

➡ _____

07

> 침대 위에서 뛰지 마.
> (jump, the bed, on, don't)

➡ _____

08 빈칸에 들어갈 말이 <u>다른</u> 하나는?

① _____ clever the dog is!

② _____ quickly she speaks!

③ _____ expensive the sofa is!

④ _____ funny stories they are!

09 문장에서 생략할 수 있는 부분은?

> What a huge cake it is!

① What

② a

③ cake

④ it is

[10-11] 다음 중 <u>틀린</u> 문장을 고르시오.

10 ① How well he swims!

② How sweet are you!

③ What long hair she has!

④ What a small room it is!

11 ① Don't complain.

② Be nice to your sister.

③ Please sits on this chair.

④ Don't watch too much TV.

[12-13] 우리말을 영어로 바르게 옮긴 것을 고르시오.

12
> 서울은 참 큰 도시구나!

① How big city Seoul is!

② How a big city Seoul is!

③ What big a city Seoul is!

④ What a big city Seoul is!

13
> 네 시간을 낭비하지 마.

① Not waste your time.

② Waste not your time.

③ Don't waste your time.

④ You don't waste your time.

서술형

[14-15] 주어진 말을 이용하여 우리말을 영어로 바꿔 쓰시오.

14
> 그 경기는 참 흥미진진하구나!
> (how, exciting, the game)

➡ _____

15
> 학교에 다시는 늦지 마. (late for, again)

➡ _____

Grammar +Plus Writing

START

3

DARAKWON

Grammar +Plus Writing

START

WORKBOOK 3

A 밑줄 친 부분이 맞으면 O를 쓰고, <u>틀리면</u> 바르게 고치세요.

1 The water feels <u>coldly</u>. → _____

2 Lucy lent <u>her roommate</u> a dress. → _____

3 Who sent <u>your</u> this gift? → _____

4 The music sounds <u>lively</u>. → _____

5 This cake tastes <u>delicious</u>. → _____

6 The dress looks <u>elegantly</u>. → _____

7 The wind feels <u>cool</u> on a hot day. → _____

8 My brother lent <u>mine</u> his car. → _____

9 The blue cheese smells <u>strongly</u>. → _____

10 The sunset looks <u>beautifully</u>. → _____

11 Janet wrote <u>our</u> a letter. → _____

12 I gave <u>my brother</u> my old textbook. → _____

13 Jason showed <u>his friend</u> a new recipe. → _____

14 Joanne sent <u>her niece's</u> a birthday card. → _____

15 The lemonade tastes <u>sour</u>. → _____

Answer Key p.21

B 주어진 말을 바르게 배열하여 문장을 완성하세요.

1 그 빵은 버터향이 난다. (buttery, the bread, smells)

➡ _____

2 너는 그녀에게 돈을 빌려 줬니? (lend, did, her, you, some money)

➡ _____

3 그 아이스크림은 달콤하다. (sweet, tastes, the ice cream)

➡ _____

4 빗소리가 부드럽게 들린다. (soft, sounds, the rain)

➡ _____

5 나는 나의 사촌에게 생일 초대장을 보냈다. (I, a birthday invitation, my cousin, sent)

➡ _____

6 비 온 뒤에 무지개가 형형색색으로 보인다. (the rainbow, colorful, after the rain, looks)

➡ _____

7 Grace는 친구에게 색이 화려한 팔찌를 주었다. (a colorful bracelet, her friend, Grace, gave)

➡ _____

8 그녀는 나에게 그녀의 고양이 사진을 보여 주었다. (showed, her cat, me, she, a photo of)

➡ _____

9 바람이 부드럽고 시원하게 느껴진다. (the breeze, gentle, cool, and, feels)

➡ _____

10 Harry는 선생님께 이메일을 썼다. (an email, wrote, Harry, his teacher)

➡ _____

UNIT 02 목적보어를 갖는 동사

A ( ) 안에서 알맞은 것을 고르세요.

1 Ted always makes his room (neat, neatly).

2 She named (her cat, her cat's) Buddy.

3 They elected (Angela, Angela's) the class president.

4 The raincoats keep (we, us) dry.

5 Their teamwork made the project (a success, successfully).

6 I found the garden (beautifully, beautiful).

7 Training made (her, she) a skilled dancer.

8 We found the puzzle (difficulty, difficult).

9 The song made (she, her) a famous singer.

10 Ann called (her kitten, her kitten's) Mitten.

11 My brother left the door (open, opening).

12 Practice made (he, him) a great player.

13 The teacher makes the lesson (interesting, interestingly).

14 We elected Mr. Cooper (the mayor's, the mayor).

15 The music made people (happy, happily).

Answer Key p.21

B 주어진 말을 이용하여 우리말을 영어로 바꿔 쓰세요.

1 그 요리사는 스토브 위에 수프를 따뜻하게 두었다. (the chef, the soup, on the stove)

➡ _____

2 그 과학자는 그의 새로운 발견을 Solaris라고 이름 지었다. (the scientist, discovery)

➡ _____

3 그 컴퓨터는 업무를 효율적으로 만든다. (the tasks, efficient)

➡ _____

4 나는 그 설명서가 매우 도움이 된다고 생각했다. (the manual, very helpful)

➡ _____

5 그 사육사는 그 아기 코끼리를 Peanut이라고 이름 지었다. (the zookeeper)

➡ _____

6 나는 그 수학 시험이 어렵다고 생각했다. (the math test, difficult)

➡ _____

7 그의 창의력은 그를 훌륭한 발명가로 만들었다. (creativity, a great inventor)

➡ _____

8 우리는 우리의 선생님을 Brown 씨라고 부른다. (our teacher, Ms. Brown)

➡ _____

9 그녀는 창문을 닫힌 채로 두었다. (closed)

➡ _____

10 우리는 Michael을 팀의 주장으로 뽑았다. (the captain, of the team)

➡ _____

UNIT 01 Can / May

A

A ( ) 안에서 알맞은 것을 고르세요.

1 Don't give up. You (can, can't) do it!

2 Where is my key? I (can, can't) find it.

3 Take a coat with you. It (may, may not) be cold today.

4 (May I, Do I may) see your ID card, please?

5 Spiders (can, can't) climb walls very well.

6 I drank a lot of coffee. I (can, can't) sleep well.

7 I woke up late. I (may, may not) be late for school.

8 You are a minor. You (can, can't) drive a car.

9 You look very tired. You (may, may not) take a break.

10 Bradley is short, but he (can, can't) play basketball well.

11 He (may, may not) help us. He is very busy.

12 I hurt my leg. I (can, can't) walk to school.

13 Where is your doll? – It (may, doesn't may) be in the box.

14 You (may, may not) use my car today. I have to use it.

15 I have an appointment. (May I, Do I may) leave work early?

Answer Key p.21

B 주어진 말을 이용하여 우리말을 영어로 바꿔 쓰세요.

1 나의 여동생은 프랑스어를 유창하게 말할 수 있다. (French, fluently)

➡ _____

2 당신은 당신의 차를 지정된 지역에 주차해도 좋아요. (in the designated area)

➡ _____

3 내가 너의 숙제를 도와 줄 수 있어. (with your homework)

➡ _____

4 우리는 공원에서 소풍을 할 수 있어. (have a picnic)

➡ _____

5 나는 겨울방학 동안 이탈리아에 갈지도 모른다. (during winter vacation)

➡ _____

6 그녀는 파티에 늦게 도착할지도 모른다. (late to the party)

➡ _____

7 우리는 새 차를 살 여유가 없다. (can't afford to)

➡ _____

8 이 오래된 차는 고장 날지도 모른다. (break down)

➡ _____

9 그녀는 맛있는 케이크를 만들 수 있니? (bake, delicious cakes)

➡ _____

10 제가 이 업무에 당신의 도움을 받을 수 있을까요? (have your assistance, with this task)

➡ _____

Must / Have to

A ( ) 안에서 알맞은 것을 고르세요.

1   The test is tomorrow. I (must, mustn't) study tonight.

2   The baby is sleeping. You (must, don't have to) be quiet.

3   The battery is low. I (must, don't have to) charge my phone.

4   She is wearing a coat. It (must, has to) be cold outside.

5   The store is closed today. We (must, don't have to) shop tomorrow.

6   The door is locked. You (have to, mustn't) use the key.

7   The road is slippery. Drivers (must, don't have to) be careful.

8   He is carrying a suitcase. He (must, has to) be traveling.

9   The restaurant is full. The food (must, has to) be good.

10   You look tired. You (have to, mustn't) go to bed now.

11   The oven is hot. You (must, mustn't) touch it.

12   He (must, mustn't) wear a helmet when he rides a bicycle.

13   It is raining outside. You (have to, don't have to) take an umbrella.

14   Take your time. You (must, don't have to) hurry.

15   The piano is heavy. We (have to, don't have to) ask for help.

Answer Key p.22

B 주어진 말을 이용하여 우리말을 영어로 바꿔 쓰세요.

1 너는 오후 5시까지 너의 숙제를 끝내야 한다. (finish, by 5:00 p.m.)

➡ _____

2 그들은 소풍을 가는 중일 것이다. (be going on a picnic)

➡ _____

3 너는 정크푸드를 너무 많이 먹어서는 안 된다. (too much junk food)

➡ _____

4 우리는 오전 8시까지 공항에 있어야 한다. (at the airport, by 8:00 a.m.)

➡ _____

5 그들은 학교에 교복을 입고 가야만 하니? (wear uniforms to school)

➡ _____

6 사람들은 이 지역에서 담배를 피워서는 안 된다. (smoke, in this area)

➡ _____

7 우리는 일찍 떠나야만 한다. (leave)

➡ _____

8 그는 시험을 준비하는 중일 것이다. (be preparing for an exam)

➡ _____

9 학생들은 수업 중에 그들의 전화기를 사용해서는 안 된다. (during class)

➡ _____

10 그는 내일 일찍 일어날 필요가 없다. (wake up, early tomorrow)

➡ _____

비교급과 최상급: 규칙 변화

A 주어진 단어의 비교급과 최상급을 쓰세요.

1 hard _____ _____

2 lazy _____ _____

3 young _____ _____

4 close _____ _____

5 loud _____ _____

6 dirty _____ _____

7 slow _____ _____

8 nice _____ _____

9 slim _____ _____

10 brave _____ _____

11 busy _____ _____

12 warm _____ _____

13 fat _____ _____

14 popular _____ _____

15 interesting _____ _____

B 주어진 말을 이용하여 우리말과 같은 뜻이 되도록 빈칸을 완성하세요.

1 아빠는 엄마보다 키가 더 크다. (tall)

→ My dad is _____ _____ my mom.

2 축구는 전 세계적으로 가장 인기있는 스포츠이다. (popular)

→ Soccer is _____ _____ _____ sport worldwide.

3 내 자전거는 너의 것보다 더 비싸다. (expensive)

→ My bicycle is _____ _____ _____ yours.

4 내 가방이 교실에서 가장 무겁다. (heavy)

→ My backpack is _____ _____ in the class.

5 올해 여름은 작년보다 더 덥다. (hot)

→ This summer is _____ _____ last year.

6 치타는 육상에서 가장 빠른 동물이다. (fast)

→ Cheetahs are _____ _____ animals on land.

7 이것은 시중에 나와있는 가장 최신형 장난감이다. (new)

→ This is _____ _____ toy on the market.

8 금성이 화성보다 더 크다. (big)

→ Venus is _____ _____ Mars.

9 나의 할아버지는 우리 식구 중에서 가장 나이가 많은 분이다. (old)

→ My grandfather is _____ _____ person in my family.

10 그 파란색 셔츠는 빨간색 셔츠보다 더 부드럽다. (soft)

→ The blue shirt is _____ _____ the red one.

A ( ) 안에서 알맞은 것을 고르세요.

1 I have (little, less, least) candy than my friend.

2 Her painting is prettier and (many, more, most) colorful than mine.

3 Apples are (good, better, best) for your health.

4 She is (much, more, most) taller than her younger brother.

5 Snakes are (little, less, least) friendly than rabbits.

6 We have (many, more, most) books in our school library.

7 The blue crayon is my (little, less, least) favorite color.

8 Breaking my toy was bad, but breaking my bicycle was (bad, worse, worst).

9 I have (many, more, most) stickers than my brother does.

10 Among all deserts, ice cream is the (good, better, best).

11 The noise is getting (loud, louder, loudest) and (loud, louder, loudest)

12 He is the (little, less, least) popular student in the class.

13 My dad's pancakes are (much, more, most) tastier than my mom's.

14 My brother's drawing is (good, better, best) than mine.

15 He is one of the (fast, faster, fastest) runners in the world.

Answer Key p.22

B 주어진 말을 이용하여 우리말을 영어로 바꿔 쓰세요.

1   다른 사람을 돕는 것은 좋은 일이다. (helping others, thing)

   ➡ _____

2   독수리는 하늘에서 가장 빠른 새들 중 하나이다. (the eagle, in the sky)

   ➡ _____

3   나의 여동생은 나보다 더 적은 숙제를 가지고 있다. (homework, I do)

   ➡ _____

4   나는 바구니에 오렌지보다 사과를 더 많이 가지고 있다. (in the basket)

   ➡ _____

5   그 영화의 가장 흥미롭지 않은 부분은 시작 부분이었다. (exciting part, the beginning)

   ➡ _____

6   나는 Ryan보다 더 나쁜 성적을 받았다. (receive, grade)

   ➡ _____

7   주전자 안의 물은 점점 더 뜨거워지고 있다. (in the pot)

   ➡ _____

8   바다는 호수보다 훨씬 더 크다. (the ocean, the lake)

   ➡ _____

9   매일 독서하는 것은 당신을 더 나은 독자로 만들 수 있다. (reading every day, reader)

   ➡ _____

10   로켓은 비행기보다 훨씬 더 빠르다. (the rocket, the airplane)

   ➡ _____

A ( ) 안에서 알맞은 전치사를 고르세요.

1 You can see the stars (at, in, on) night.

2 We will go to the theater (after, for) dinner.

3 We will have a picnic (at, in, on) Saturday.

4 Joe took a trip to Japan (for, during) summer vacation.

5 My birthday is (at, in, on) September 10.

6 We will play board games (until, from) bedtime.

7 I have a doctor's appointment (at, in, on) the afternoon.

8 I always brush my teeth (before, from) going to bed.

9 My dance practice is (from, during) 4:00 p.m. (in, to) 6:00 p.m.

10 Let's meet at the bus stop (at, in, on) the morning.

11 We will study English (for, during) an hour every day.

12 We have soccer practice (at, in, on) 5 o'clock.

13 The days become longer (at, in, on) spring.

14 My sister was born (at, in, on) 2014.

15 I will wait for you (for, until) 5 o'clock.

Answer Key p.23

B 우리말을 참고하여 밑줄 친 부분을 바르게 고쳐 문장을 다시 쓰세요.

1 We often go hiking <u>in</u> the weekend. 우리는 주말에 자주 등산을 간다.

➡ _____

2 We will be camping <u>during</u> three days. 우리는 3일 동안 캠핑을 할 것이다.

➡ _____

3 The concert is held on a summer night <u>at</u> July. 그 콘서트는 7월의 한 여름밤에 열린다.

➡ _____

4 I like to read books <u>at</u> rainy days. 나는 비 오는 날에 책 읽는 것을 좋아한다.

➡ _____

5 Please wash your hands <u>from</u> dinner. 저녁 식사 전에 손을 씻으세요.

➡ _____

6 The store's grand opening is <u>on</u> 10:00 a.m. 그 상점의 개점 행사는 오전 10시이다.

➡ _____

7 The library is open <u>for</u> Monday to Saturday. 그 도서관은 월요일부터 토요일까지 문을 연다.

➡ _____

8 I love to swim <u>for</u> hot days. 나는 더운 날에 수영하는 것을 좋아한다.

➡ _____

9 I will be on vacation in Spain <u>on</u> August. 나는 8월에 스페인에서 휴가를 보낼 것이다.

➡ _____

10 You can play outside <u>from</u> sunset. 너는 해질녘까지 밖에서 놀아도 된다.

➡ _____

A ( ) 안에서 알맞은 전치사를 고르세요.

1 The remote control is (between, on) the table.

2 The umbrella is (in, under) the chair.

3 There is a coffee shop (in front of, on) the school.

4 The chef is cooking (in, on) the kitchen.

5 Her house is (between, across from) the park.

6 There are beautiful flowers (on, in) the garden

7 The playground is (behind, between) the school and the library.

8 The cookies are (on, in) the plate.

9 The cat was sitting (on, in front of) the fireplace.

10 There is a spider (in, under) the corner.

11 The dog was hiding (behind, between) the couch.

12 The bicycle is parked (on, next to) the tree.

13 The car stopped (on, in) the mountains.

14 Our office is (on, across from) the subway station.

15 The store is located (next to, between) the bank and the post office.

Answer Key p.23

B 주어진 말을 바르게 배열하여 문장을 완성하세요.

1 그 어린이들은 수영장에서 수영을 하고 있다. (are swimming, the pool, the children, in)

➡ _____

2 그 어린이들은 집 뒤에서 놀고 있었다. (behind, were playing, the house, the children)

➡ _____

3 그 아이들은 운동장에서 축구를 하고 있다. (on, are playing, the kids, soccer, the playground)

➡ _____

4 시청 앞에 조각상이 있다. (in front of, is, there, a statue, City Hall)

➡ _____

5 나는 소파 아래에서 장난감을 찾았다. (I, the toy, the sofa, under, found)

➡ _____

6 두 집 사이에 작은 정원이 있다. (a, small, between, there, is, garden, the two houses)

➡ _____

7 그는 차고에서 그의 차를 고치고 있다. (is fixing, he, the garage, his car, in)

➡ _____

8 아빠는 내 앞에 선물 상자를 놓아 두었다. (placed, me, in front of, the gift box, my dad)

➡ _____

9 그 펜은 공책 옆에 있다. (is, the pen, the notebook, next to)

➡ _____

10 그 호텔 건너편에 편의점이 있다. (the hotel, there, a convenience store, across from, is)

➡ _____

A   ( ) 안에서 알맞은 접속사를 고르세요.

1   The weather is sunny (and, but) warm.

2   The concert was loud, (but, so) it was a lot of fun.

3   Sarah is a great dancer (and, but) skilled pianist.

4   I finished my chores, (and, or) I watched a movie.

5   Do you want to wear the red shirt (but, or) the blue one?

6   We wanted to go out, (and, but) it started raining.

7   Joanne studied hard, (or, so) she passed the exam.

8   I set the alarm, (but, or) I overslept again.

9   You can walk to the store, (and, or) you can take your bicycle.

10   They packed their bags, (and, but) they went to the airport.

11   The team trained hard, (but, so) they could win the championship.

12   The cake is delicious (but, or) expensive.

13   She is hardworking, (and, but) she always gives her best.

14   I want to travel to Europe (but, or) Asia.

15   She lived in the USA, (but, so) she speaks English well.

B 우리말을 참고하여 밑줄 친 부분을 바르게 고쳐 문장을 다시 쓰세요.

1 She is skilled <u>but</u> dedicated. 그녀는 능숙하고 헌신적이다.

➡ _____

2 My laptop is powerful <u>or</u> heavy. 내 노트북 컴퓨터는 강력하지만 무겁다.

➡ _____

3 Ted is reading a book, <u>but</u> I am studying. Ted는 독서 중이고, 나는 공부하는 중이다.

➡ _____

4 Are you interested in painting <u>and</u> sculpture? 너는 회화에 관심있니 조각에 관심있니?

➡ _____

5 The food was delicious, <u>and</u> I was hungry. 음식이 맛있었거나, 내가 배고팠던 것이다.

➡ _____

6 The movie was long <u>or</u> exciting. 그 영화는 길었지만 흥미로웠다.

➡ _____

7 She is talented at singing <u>but</u> dancing. 그녀는 노래와 춤에 재능이 있다.

➡ _____

8 The coffee was bitter, <u>or</u> I put some sugar in it. 그 커피가 써서, 나는 설탕을 넣었다.

➡ _____

9 Do you want to have pizza <u>and</u> pasta? 너는 피자를 원하니 파스타를 원하니?

➡ _____

10 He is tired, <u>or</u> he needs to finish his work. 그는 지쳤지만, 그의 일을 끝내야 한다.

➡ _____

종속 접속사

A 보기에서 알맞은 말을 골라 문장을 완성하세요.

after the concert was over	after we bake cookies
because I was thirsty	because it was expensive
before I go for a run	before I leave for school
if it is sunny	if you are patient
when the soil feels dry	when it is raining outside

1 I check my backpack _____.

2 _____, we enjoy them with milk.

3 _____, I drank a glass of orange juice.

4 _____, we can go to the park.

5 People clapped their hands _____.

6 I water the plants _____.

7 I tie my shoelaces _____.

8 You can learn to play the piano _____.

9 I didn't buy the laptop _____.

10 Jean wears her raincoat _____.

Answer Key p.23

B 주어진 말을 이용하여 우리말을 영어로 바꿔 쓰세요.

1 해가 질 때, 하늘은 오렌지색과 핑크색으로 변한다. (the sun sets, turns orange and pink)

→ _____

2 네가 걷는다면 너는 학교에 늦을 것이다. (late for school, walk)

→ _____

3 TV를 보기 전에 너는 숙제를 해야만 한다. (have to, your homework, watch TV)

→ _____

4 날씨가 더웠기 때문에, 나는 선풍기를 틀었다. (the weather, hot, turned on, the fan)

→ _____

5 연극이 끝난 후에, 배우들은 관객에게 인사했다. (the actors, greeted, the audience)

→ _____

6 밤하늘이 맑을 때 별들이 반짝인다. (twinkle, clear)

→ _____

7 그것이 나를 안전하게 지켜주기 때문에 나는 항상 안전벨트를 맨다. (wear, keep, safe)

→ _____

8 우리가 규칙적으로 운동한다면, 우리의 몸은 강해진다. (exercise regularly, become strong)

→ _____

9 우리가 전등을 끈 후에, 우리는 교실을 떠났다. (turned off the lights, left the classroom)

→ _____

10 파티가 시작하기 전에, 우리는 방을 장식했다. (decorate the room)

→ _____

A ( ) 안에서 알맞은 것을 고르세요.

1 (What, How) a genius idea that is!

2 (What, How) tall the man is!

3 (What, How) an amazing singer she is!

4 (What, How) a clever idea it is!

5 (What, How) gently the wind blows!

6 (What, How) a nice car you drive!

7 (What, How) fantastic that movie is!

8 (What, How) cute puppies they are!

9 (What, How) a long neck the giraffe has!

10 (What, How) delicious this dish is!

11 (What, How) colorful butterflies they are!

12 (What, How) fast he runs!

13 (What, How) quietly the cat walks!

14 (What, How) a brave firefighter he is!

15 (What, How) carefully she drives!

Answer Key p.24

B 주어진 말을 바르게 배열하여 문장을 완성하세요.

1 그들은 참 뛰어난 운동선수들이구나! (great, are, athletes, they, what)

➡ _____

2 달팽이가 참 느리게 움직이는구나! (how, the snail, slowly, moves)

➡ _____

3 참 슬픈 소식이구나! (sad, it, is, what, news)

➡ _____

4 그것은 참 높은 건물이구나! (is, tall, what, a, building, it)

➡ _____

5 그 경기는 참 흥미롭구나! (the game, exciting, how, is)

➡ _____

6 그것은 참 편안한 소파구나! (what, it, sofa, a, is, comfortable)

➡ _____

7 별들이 참 아름답구나! (beautiful, are, how, the stars)

➡ _____

8 이 침대는 참 아늑하구나! (this bed, how, cozy, is)

➡ _____

9 너는 참 멋진 목소리를 가지고 있구나! (what, have, incredible, voice, you, an)

➡ _____

10 그들은 파티에서 참 행복하게 춤을 추었구나! (danced, how, they, at the party, happily)

➡ _____

A 보기에서 알맞은 말을 골라 문장을 완성하세요.

be honest	be noisy	call	check
close	feed	finish	open
read	run	waste	wear

1 _____ the door, please. It's cold outside.

2 Please _____ your hard hat.

3 _____ your pet on time.

4 _____ with your friends.

5 _____ me when you get home.

6 Please _____ the instructions carefully.

7 Please _____ your spelling and grammar.

8 _____ your homework first.

9 Don't _____ in the hallway.

10 Don't _____ your time on games.

11 Don't _____. Be quiet in the library.

12 Don't _____ that box, please.

Answer Key p.24

B 주어진 말을 바르게 배열하여 문장을 완성하세요.

1 더 크게 얘기해 주세요. (speak, please, louder)

    ➡ _____

2 슬퍼하지 마. 항상 희망은 있어. (don't, sad, hope, be, is, always, there)

    ➡ _____

3 네가 실수할 때에는 사과해라. (apologize, when, make, a mistake, you)

    ➡ _____

4 당신의 차를 여기에 주차하지 마세요. (don't, car, please, park, here, your)

    ➡ _____

5 길을 건너기 전에 양쪽을 확인해라. (look, before, ways, crossing, both, the street)

    ➡ _____

6 거리에 쓰레기를 버리지 마. (don't, on the street, litter)

    ➡ _____

7 너의 친구들과 장난감을 같이 가지고 놀아라. (share, your friends, with, your toys)

    ➡ _____

8 손톱을 깨물지 마. 그것은 나쁜 습관이야. (don't, nails, it's, a bad habit, bite, your)

    ➡ _____

9 강의에 집중해 주세요. (please, the lecture, pay attention to)

    ➡ _____

10 그 종이를 버리지 마세요. (don't, that paper, please, throw away)

    ➡ _____

Chapter 01

다음 단어들을 잘 듣고 따라 쓴 후 그 뜻을 쓰세요.

UNIT 01 감각동사/수여동사

단어	뜻	단어 쓰기	뜻 쓰기
01 honey	명 꿀		
02 lend	동 빌려주다		
03 show	동 보여주다		
04 graduation	명 졸업		
05 ceremony	명 의식, 식		
06 awful	형 끔찍한, 지독한		
07 voice	명 목소리		
08 silk	명 비단, 실크		
09 blouse	명 블라우스		
10 busy	형 바쁜		
11 shampoo	명 샴푸		
12 tablet	명 태블릿 컴퓨터		
13 clerk	명 점원		
14 package	명 소포		
15 company	명 회사		
16 bill	명 고지서, 청구서		
17 salad	명 샐러드		
18 pineapple	명 파인애플		

단어	뜻	단어 쓰기	뜻 쓰기
19 flute	명 플루트		
20 Parents' Day	명 어버이날		
21 text message	명 문자메시지		
22 surprised	형 놀란		
23 lonely	형 외로운		
24 pronunciation	명 발음		
25 perfect	형 완벽한		
26 pocket money	명 용돈		
27 comic book	명 만화책		
28 ID card	명 신분증		
29 depressed	형 우울한		
30 result	명 결과		

UNIT 02 목적보어를 갖는 동사

단어	뜻	단어 쓰기	뜻 쓰기
01 keep	동 유지하다		
02 awake	형 깨어 있는		
03 a little	부 조금, 약간		
04 mosquito	명 모기		
05 name	명 이름 동 이름 짓다		
06 elect	동 선출하다		
07 president	명 대통령, 회장 class president 반장		

08	clown	명 광대		
09	part-time job	명 시간제 근무, 아르바이트		
10	situation	명 상황		
11	goldfish	명 금붕어		
12	invention	명 발명(품)		
13	millionaire	명 백만장자		
14	hamster	명 햄스터		
15	better	형 더 나은		
16	chairman	명 의장, 회장		
17	flight	명 비행		
18	crossword puzzle	명 낱말 맞추기 게임		
19	bear	명 곰		
20	leader	명 리더, 지도자		
21	behavior	명 행동		
22	unlocked	형 잠겨있지 않은		
23	fireplace	명 벽난로		
24	teen	형 10대의		
25	idol	명 우상		
26	novel	명 소설		
27	ice	명 얼음		
28	duck	명 오리		
29	spicy	형 매운, 맛이 강한		
30	rudeness	명 무례함		

Chapter 02

다음 단어들을 잘 듣고 따라 쓴 후 그 뜻을 쓰세요.

UNIT 01 Can / May

단어	뜻	단어 쓰기	뜻 쓰기
01 can	~할 수 있다		
02 may	~일지도 모른다; ~해도 좋다		
03 by bus	버스로		
04 penguin	명 펭귄		
05 fly	동 날다		
06 file	명 파일, 서류철		
07 Korean	명 한국어 형 한국인		
08 another	형 또 하나(의)		
09 squirrel	명 다람쥐		
10 language	명 언어		
11 crawl	동 (엎드려) 기다		
12 recognize	동 알아보다		
13 handwriting	명 필체		
14 musical instrument	명 악기		
15 on foot	걸어서, 도보로		
16 loud	형 시끄러운		
17 slipper	명 슬리퍼, 실내화		
18 later	부 나중에 later today 오늘 늦게		

19 **driver's license**	명 운전 면허(증)		
20 **press**	동 누르다		
21 **seat**	명 자리, 좌석 **take a seat** 자리에 앉다		
22 **violin**	명 바이올린 **play the violin** 바이올린을 연주하다		
23 **airplane**	명 비행기		
24 **true**	형 사실인		
25 **Chinese**	명 중국어; 중국인		
26 **believe**	동 믿다		
27 **Thailand**	명 태국		
28 **ice cream**	명 아이스크림		
29 **hallway**	명 복도		
30 **passport**	명 여권		

UNIT 02 Must / Have to

단어	뜻	단어 쓰기	뜻 쓰기
01 **must**	~해야 한다; ~임에 틀림없다		
02 **have to**	~해야 한다		
03 **follow**	동 따르다		
04 **rule**	명 규칙		
05 **hurry**	동 서두르다		
06 **downtown**	부 시내에		
07 **seatbelt**	명 안전벨트		

08 **garbage**	명 쓰레기 take out the garbage 쓰레기를 버리다		
09 **fill out**	작성하다		
10 **form**	명 양식		
11 **deep**	형 깊은		
12 **fire department**	명 소방서, 소방대		
13 **stay up**	안 자다, 깨어 있다		
14 **harmful**	형 해로운		
15 **yell**	동 소리지르다		
16 **back**	명 등, 허리		
17 **lonely**	형 외로운		
18 **junk food**	명 정크 푸드		
19 **smoke**	동 담배를 피우다		
20 **copy**	동 복사하다; 베끼다		
21 **obey**	동 따르다, 순종하다		
22 **during**	~ 동안, ~ 중에		
23 **rest**	명 휴식 get some rest 휴식을 취하다		
24 **take care of**	~을 돌보다		
25 **weight**	명 무게, 체중 lose weight 살을 빼다		
26 **fine**	명 벌금 pay a fine 벌금을 내다		
27 **chess**	명 체스 play chess 체스를 하다		
28 **supermarket**	명 슈퍼마켓		
29 **pants**	명 바지		
30 **fit**	동 (꼭) 맞다		

Chapter 03

다음 단어들을 잘 듣고 따라 쓴 후 그 뜻을 쓰세요.

UNIT 01 비교급과 최상급: 규칙 변화

단어	뜻	단어 쓰기	뜻 쓰기
01 long	형 (길이·거리가) 긴		
02 nice	형 좋은, 멋진		
03 pretty	형 예쁜		
04 chair	명 의자		
05 comfortable	형 편안한		
06 year	명 해, 년		
07 banana	명 바나나		
08 August	명 8월		
09 witch	명 마녀		
10 large	형 큰		
11 cheap	형 (값이) 싼		
12 thin	형 얇은; 마른		
13 useful	형 유용한		
14 attractive	형 매력적인		
15 hill	명 언덕		
16 lucky	형 운이 좋은		
17 life	명 생명; 삶		
18 February	명 2월		

19 short	형 짧은; 키가 작은		
20 intelligent	형 지적인		
21 tulip	명 튤립		
22 bracelet	명 팔찌		
23 score	명 점수		
24 January	명 1월		
25 neighborhood	명 이웃, 동네		
26 health	명 건강		
27 peaceful	형 평화로운		
28 diary	명 일기(장)		
29 neat	형 정돈된, 단정한		
30 moon	명 달		

UNIT 02 비교급과 최상급: 불규칙 변화

단어	뜻	단어 쓰기	뜻 쓰기
01 worse	형 더 나쁜		
02 worst	형 가장 나쁜		
03 more	형 더 많은		
04 most	형 가장 많은		
05 less	형 더 적은		
06 least	형 가장 적은		
07 player	명 선수		

08	team	명 팀, 단체		
09	rich	형 부유한		
10	worker	명 일꾼		
11	choose	동 선택하다, 고르다		
12	hotel	명 호텔		
13	green	명 초록색		
14	milk	명 우유		
15	dress	명 드레스, 원피스		
16	silver	명 은		
17	electric car	명 전기 자동차		
18	film	명 영화 (= movie)		
19	Arabic	명 아랍어		
20	Western	형 서양의		
21	shop	명 가게, 상점		
22	outgoing	형 외향적인		
23	allowance	명 용돈 (= pocket money)		
24	impressive	형 인상적인		
25	speech	명 연설		
26	choir	명 합창단		
27	laptop	명 노트북		
28	bakery	명 빵집, 제과점		
29	pair	명 짝, 한 벌 a pair of shoes 신발 한 켤레		
30	sunflower	명 해바라기		

Chapter 04

UNIT 01 시간의 전치사

단어	뜻	단어 쓰기	뜻 쓰기
01 **noon**	명 정오, 낮 12시		
02 **Monday**	명 월요일		
03 **Children's Day**	명 어린이날		
04 **Friday**	명 금요일		
05 **Thursday**	명 목요일		
06 **before**	전 ~ 전에		
07 **for**	전 ~ 동안		
08 **hour**	명 시간		
09 **July**	명 7월		
10 **October**	명 10월		
11 **o'clock**	명 시 at five o'clock 5시에		
12 **snowball fight**	명 눈싸움 have a snowball fight 눈싸움을 하다		
13 **September**	명 9월		
14 **almost**	부 거의		
15 **fall asleep**	잠들다		
16 **thirty**	명 30, 서른		
17 **half**	명 반, 절반 half an hour 30분		
18 **owl**	명 올빼미, 부엉이		

19	bat	명 박쥐		
20	day	명 하루; 낮; 요일		
21	second	형 두 번째의		
22	go out	(불·전깃불이) 꺼지다, 나가다		
23	storm	명 폭풍, 폭풍우		
24	mall	명 쇼핑몰		
25	place	명 장소		
26	holiday	명 휴가; 휴일		
27	there	부 거기에(서), 그곳에(서)		
28	abroad	부 해외에, 해외로 study abroad 유학하다		
29	New Year's Day	명 1월 1일, 새해 첫날		
30	bloom	동 꽃이 피다		

UNIT 02 장소의 전치사

단어		뜻	단어 쓰기	뜻 쓰기
01	door	명 문		
02	ship	명 배		
03	behind	전 ~ 뒤에		
04	between	전 ~ 사이에 between A and B A와 B 사이에		
05	across from	전 ~의 맞은편에		
06	market	명 시장		
07	bicycle	명 자전거		

08	truck	명 트럭, 화물차		
09	hang	동 걸다, 매달다		
10	fifth	형 다섯 번째의 on the fifth floor 5층에		
11	broom	명 빗자루		
12	bench	명 벤치, 긴 의자		
13	twelve	명 12, 열둘		
14	tent	명 텐트		
15	ground	명 땅 on the ground 땅에		
16	café	명 카페		
17	cheek	명 볼, 뺨		
18	sea	명 바다		
19	hide	동 숨다		
20	face	명 얼굴		
21	stain	명 얼룩		
22	basket	명 바구니		
23	hair salon	명 미용실		
24	relax	동 쉬다, 휴식을 취하다		
25	beach umbrella	명 파라솔		
26	police station	명 경찰서		
27	fire station	명 소방서		
28	stationery store	명 문구점		
29	pot	명 화분; 냄비		
30	mirror	명 거울		

UNIT 01 등위 접속사

단어	뜻	단어 쓰기	뜻 쓰기
01 and	접 그리고		
02 but	접 그러나		
03 or	접 또는		
04 so	접 그래서		
05 king	명 왕		
06 unhappy	형 불행한		
07 pear	명 배		
08 shiny	형 빛나는		
09 grape	명 포도		
10 mango	명 망고		
11 read	동 읽다		
12 cell phone	명 휴대폰 (= cellular phone)		
13 pasta	명 파스타		
14 beef	명 쇠고기		
15 shorts	명 반바지		
16 unhealthy	형 건강하지 못한; 건강에 해로운		
17 flag	명 기, 깃발		
18 white	명 흰색 형 흰색의		

19	cash	몡 현금		
20	credit card	몡 신용카드		
21	be good at	~을 잘하다		
22	yard	몡 마당, 뜰		
23	heater	몡 난방기, 히터 turn on the heater 히터를 켜다		
24	get off	내리다, 하차하다		
25	put on	~을 입다		
26	coat	몡 코트, 외투		
27	tidy	혱 잘 정돈된		
28	forgetful	혱 잘 잊는, 건망증이 있는		
29	excellent	혱 훌륭한		
30	snake	몡 뱀		

UNIT 02 종속 접속사

단어		뜻	단어 쓰기	뜻 쓰기
01	dry	혱 마른 동 말리다		
02	shy	혱 부끄럼을 많이 타는		
03	if	쩝 만약		
04	gain	동 쌓다, 늘다 gain weight 체중이 늘다		
05	fan	몡 선풍기		
06	cute	혱 귀여운		
07	map	몡 지도		

08	left	명 왼쪽		
09	marathon	명 마라톤		
10	alarm clock	명 자명종		
11	popcorn	명 팝콘		
12	get lost	길을 잃다		
13	coffee	명 커피		
14	snowman	명 눈사람		
15	crowded	형 붐비는, 복잡한		
16	price	명 가격		
17	go down	(가격·기온 등이) 내려가다		
18	spinach	명 시금치		
19	both	양쪽 모두		
20	way	명 길		
21	regularly	부 규칙적으로		
22	hamburger	명 햄버거		
23	snack	명 간식		
24	refreshed	형 상쾌한		
25	book	명 책 동 예약하다		
26	pray	동 기도하다		
27	high school	명 고등학교		
28	textbook	명 교과서		
29	cancel	동 취소하다		
30	cookie	명 쿠키		

Chapter 06

다음 단어들을 잘 듣고 따라 쓴 후 그 뜻을 쓰세요.

UNIT 01 감탄문

단어	뜻	단어 쓰기	뜻 쓰기
01 girl	명 소녀		
02 boy	명 소년		
03 man	명 남자		
04 woman	명 여자		
05 rude	형 무례한		
06 stupid	형 어리석은, 멍청한		
07 beautifully	부 아름답게		
08 cake	명 케이크		
09 family	명 가족		
10 computer	명 컴퓨터		
11 slow	형 느린		
12 badly	부 나쁘게, 잘 못하는		
13 rabbit	명 토끼		
14 run away	달아나다, 도망치다		
15 jacket	명 재킷		
16 sunset	명 노을, 해질녘		
17 messy	형 지저분한		
18 have a great time	즐거운 시간을 보내다		

단어	뜻	단어 쓰기	뜻 쓰기
19 house	명 집, 주택		
20 friend	명 친구		
21 French	명 프랑스어; 프랑스인		
22 amazing	형 놀라운		
23 story	명 이야기		
24 swan	명 백조		
25 landscape	명 풍경		
26 hat	명 모자		
27 ending	명 결말		
28 surprising	형 놀라운		
29 news	명 소식, 뉴스		
30 car	명 차, 승용차		

UNIT 02 명령문

단어	뜻	단어 쓰기	뜻 쓰기
01 please	부 부디, 제발		
02 quiet	형 조용한		
03 careful	형 조심하는		
04 turn up	(소리·온도 등을) 높이다		
05 turn down	(소리·온도 등을) 낮추다		
06 volume	명 음량, 볼륨		
07 table	명 탁자		

08	brother	뗑 형제		
09	wash the dishes	설거지를 하다		
10	touch	뙕 만지다		
11	artwork	뗑 예술품		
12	mess	뗑 엉망인 상태 make a mess 어지럽히다		
13	swim	뙕 수영하다		
14	ready	뙝 준비된		
15	yet	뙖 아직		
16	page	뗑 쪽, 면		
17	road	뗑 길		
18	icy	뙝 얼음에 뒤덮인		
19	piano	뗑 피아노		
20	thing	뗑 물건, 사물		
21	energy	뗑 에너지		
22	put away	치우다		
23	take off	(옷·신발 등을) 벗다		
24	indoors	뙖 실내에서		
25	sign	뙕 서명하다		
26	have fun	재미있게 놀다		
27	sister	뗑 자매		
28	huge	뙝 거대한		
29	complain	뙕 불평하다		
30	waste	뙕 낭비하다		

Grammar
+Plus Writing
START

Grammar +Plus Writing START

Grammar Plus Writing START 시리즈는 초등학생 및 중학생이 알아야 할 기초 영문법을 쉽고 재미있게 공부하며, 문법과 쓰기의 기초를 탄탄히 다지는 것은 물론 영어 내신과 서술형 시험 대비에도 최적인 문법·쓰기 교재입니다.

초등 및 중등 교과 과정의 기초 영문법

Grammar Plus Writing START 시리즈

중등 교과 과정의 필수 영문법

Grammar Plus Writing 시리즈

온라인 부가자료 | www.darakwon.co.kr
다락원 홈페이지에서 본 교재의 상세 정보와 부가학습 자료를 이용하실 수 있습니다.

64740

9 788927 780700

ISBN 978-89-277-8070-0
978-89-277-8067-0 (set)
가격 14,000원

Grammar +Plus Writing

START

ANSWER KEY 3

Chapter 01 동사의 종류

UNIT 01 감각동사 / 수여동사

PRACTICE 1   p.10

1 tastes	**2** sounds
3 feel	**4** looks

해설
감각동사는 feel(기분[촉감]이 ~하다), look(~하게 보이다),
taste(~한 맛이 나다), smell(~한 냄새가 나다), sound(~하게
들리다)처럼 감각과 관련한 동사들로, 뒤에 형용사가 온다.

PRACTICE 2   p.11

1 to her	**2** to him
3 to Bill	**4** to us

해설
수여동사는 간접목적어(~에게)와 직접목적어(~을/를)에 해당하
는 두 개의 목적어를 갖는 동사로, 수여동사 give, send, show,
lend, write 등은 「수여동사+간접목적어+직접목적어」 또는
「수여동사+직접목적어+to+간접목적어」 형태로 쓸 수 있다.

문법 쏙쏙   pp.12~13

A

1 new	**2** interesting	**3** sweet
4 heavy	**5** angry	**6** good
7 beautiful	**8** salty	**9** happy
10 tasted	**11** felt	**12** sounds
13 feels	**14** looked	**15** smells

해설
1-9 ▶ feel, look, taste, smell, sound와 같은 감각동사 뒤에는
보어로 형용사가 온다.
10 ▶ '~한 맛이 나다'는 「taste+형용사」로 나타낸다.
11, 13 ▶ '기분[촉감]이 ~하다'는 「feel+형용사」로 나타낸다.
12 ▶ '~하게 들리다'는 「sound+형용사」로 나타낸다.
14 ▶ '~하게 보이다'는 「look+형용사」로 나타낸다.
15 ▶ '~한 냄새가 나다'는 「smell+형용사」로 나타낸다.

B

1 his tablet to me

2 a birthday card to her father

3 some shirts to me

4 this package to you

5 his guitar to her

6 his old school uniform to me

7 my best wishes to him

8 a poem to her boyfriend

9 a picture of his baby to me

10 a phone bill to me

해설
수여동사 give, send, show, lend, write 등은 「수여동사+간
접목적어+직접목적어」 또는 「수여동사+직접목적어+to+간접
목적어」 형태로 쓸 수 있다.

영작 술술   pp.14~15

A

1 We felt tired after the test.

2 The salad looks fresh.

3 The pineapple tastes sweet.

4 The flute sounds beautiful.

5 The carpet smells bad.

6 He gave me a free movie ticket.

7 Joe showed us a photo of his family.

8 I lent my friend a book.

9 I wrote my parents a letter on Parents' Day.

10 I sent a text message to Jane.

B

1 They looked surprised at the news.

2 The stew smells delicious.

3 I sometimes feel lonely.

4 Your pronunciation sounds perfect.

5 The coffee tastes sour.

6 My mom gives me pocket money.
   [My mom gives pocket money to me.]

7 Tom lent me a comic book.
   [Tom lent a comic book to me.]

8 I wrote Mike a birthday card.
   [I wrote a birthday card to Mike.]

9 I sent my friend some photos.
   [I sent some photos to my friend.]

10 The man showed the police officer his ID card.
   [The man showed his ID card to the police
   officer.]

A

1 The cheesecake tastes great.

2 I felt sick yesterday.

3 You look nice in that suit.

4 Something smells delicious.

5 She lent me her bicycle.

6 We will send the information to you.

7 He wrote a fan letter to the singer.

해설

1, 2, 3, 4 ▶ feel, look, taste, smell, sound와 같은 감각동사 뒤에는 보어로 형용사가 온다.

5, 6, 7 ▶ lend, send, write는 모두 수여동사로 「수여동사＋간접목적어＋직접목적어」 또는 「수여동사＋직접목적어＋to＋간접목적어」 형태로 쓸 수 있다.

B

1 The medicine tastes bitter.

2 Your uncle looks friendly.

3 She sounded depressed on the phone.

4 He gave me a cup of tea.

[He gave a cup of tea to me.]

5 My teacher showed me the results of the exam.[My teacher showed the results of the exam to me.]

C   1 ④   2 ③

해설

1 ▶ 형용사 good 앞에 올 수 있는 동사는 feel, look, taste, smell, sound와 같은 감각동사이다.

2 ▶ give는 수여동사로, 뒤에 「간접목적어(me)＋직접목적어(a red rose)」 또는 「직접목적어(a red rose)＋to＋간접목적어 (me)」 형태가 온다.

개념 Review

❶ 감각동사   ❷ 형용사   ❸ 간접목적어

❹ 직접목적어   ❺ to

UNIT **02** 목적보어를 갖는 동사

PRACTICE **1**   p.18

1	fat	2	boring
3	open	4	awake

해설

동사 make(만들다), keep(유지하다), leave(두다), find(생각하다, 알아채다)는 형용사를 목적보어로 취해 「동사＋목적어＋형용사」의 문장 구조를 갖는다.

PRACTICE **2**   p.19

1	call	2	elected
3	named	4	made

해설

동사 call(부르다), name(이름 짓다), make(만들다), elect(선출하다)는 명사를 목적보어로 취해 「동사＋목적어＋명사」의 문장 구조를 갖는다.

문법 쏙쏙   pp.20~21

A

1 This song makes me happy.

2 I found the book helpful.

3 Coffee keeps me awake.

4 The news made people sad.

5 Fresh vegetables keep you healthy.

6 I found the clerk very kind.

7 The clown made the party fun.

8 They left the house messy.

9 His part-time job keeps him busy.

10 They found the situation serious.

해설

1, 4, 7 ▶ '~을 …하게 만들다'는 「make＋목적어＋형용사」로 나타낸다.

2, 6, 10 ▶ '~을 …라고 생각하다'는 「find＋목적어＋형용사」로 나타낸다.

3, 5, 9 ▶ '~을 …하게 유지하다'는 「keep＋목적어＋형용사」로 나타낸다.

8 ▶ '~을 …하게 두다'는 「leave＋목적어＋형용사」로 나타낸다.

B

1 The boy named the goldfish Nemo.

2 The movie made him a famous actor.

3 We elected Minho class president.

4 They named the bridge the Golden Gate.

5 Some people call a cat a kitty.

6 The invention made the man a millionaire.

7 She named her hamster Charley.

8 They elected him the 15th president.

9 Books make me a better person.

10 We elected Mr. Kim the chairman.

1, 4, 7 ▶ '~을 …라고 이름 짓다'는 「name＋목적어＋명사」로 나타낸다.

2, 6, 9 ▶ '~을 …로 만들다'는 「make＋목적어＋명사」로 나타낸다.

3, 8, 10 ▶ '~을 …로 선출하다'는 「elect＋목적어＋명사」로 나타낸다.

5 ▶ '~을 …라고 부르다'는 「call＋목적어＋명사」로 나타낸다.

영작 술술
pp.22~23

A

1 The long flight <u>made</u> me <u>tired</u>.
2 We <u>found</u> the crossword puzzle <u>difficult</u>.
3 The noise <u>kept</u> me <u>awake</u> all night.
4 He <u>left</u> the car window <u>open</u>.
5 People <u>call</u> the bear <u>Pooh</u>.
6 Lucy <u>named</u> her dog <u>Jack</u>.
7 We <u>elected</u> <u>Mike</u> the leader of our book club.
8 I <u>found</u> his behavior <u>strange</u>.
9 This song <u>made</u> <u>him</u> a star.
10 Please <u>leave</u> me <u>alone</u>.

B

1 Rain makes me depressed.
2 The work kept me busy all day.
3 I found the science class difficult.
4 He left the door unlocked.
5 The fireplace keeps us warm.
6 I call my parents Mom and Dad.
7 They named their son David.
8 Our club elected Ryan president.
9 The lottery made him a millionaire.
10 She made her parents proud.

WRAP UP
pp.24~25

A

| 1 happy | 2 clean | 3 easy |
| 4 Violet | 5 a teen idol | 6 delicious |

1 ▶ '~을 …하게 만들다'는 「make＋목적어＋형용사」로 나타낸다.

2 ▶ '~을 …하게 유지하다'는 「keep＋목적어＋형용사」로 나타낸다.

3, 6 ▶ '~을 …라고 생각하다'는 「find＋목적어＋형용사」로 나타낸다.

4 ▶ '~을 …라고 이름 짓다'는 「name＋목적어＋명사」로 나타낸다.

5 ▶ '~을 …로 만들다'는 「make＋목적어＋명사」로 나타낸다.

B

1 He calls his wife "honey."
2 I found the painting beautiful.
3 They elected him the chairman.
4 The novel made the writer famous.
5 These socks keep your feet warm.

C

| 1 ④ | 2 ② |

1 ▶ '~을 …하게 만들다'는 「make＋목적어＋형용사」로 나타낸다. happily → happy

2 ▶ '~을 …하게 유지하다'는 「keep＋목적어(their eggs)＋형용사(warm)」로 나타낸다.

개념 Review

❶ 목적보어　　❷ 형용사　　❸ 명사

ACTUAL TEST
pp.26~27

01 ①	02 ①	03 ③	04 ②
05 ②	06 show you		
07 made, angry		08 ④	09 ③
10 ④	11 ②	12 ②	13 ①

14 They sent us a card.
[They sent a card to us.]
15 I found the work easy.

01 give는 수여동사로 뒤에 「간접목적어(me)＋직접목적어(this)」 또는 「직접목적어(this)＋to＋간접목적어(me)」 형태가 온다.

02 '~을 …라고 생각하다'는 「find＋목적어＋형용사」로 나타낸다.

03 '~한 맛이 나다'는 「taste＋형용사」이므로 부사인 terribly는 올 수 없다. terribly → terrible

04 수여동사 send의 간접목적어(~에게) 자리로 소유격인 our는 올 수 없다. our → us

05 목적보어로 형용사(cold)와 명사(a better person)를 모두 취할 수 있는 동사는 make이다.

06 '당신에게 제 그림을 보여드릴게요'라는 의미이므로 show you my drawing이 알맞다.

07 '~을 …하게 만들다'는 「make+목적어+형용사」로 나타낸다.

08 ①, ②, ③은 「수여동사+간접목적어+직접목적어」의 문장 구조이지만, ④는 「동사+목적어+형용사」의 문장 구조이다.

09 ①, ②, ④는 「동사+목적어+형용사」의 문장 구조이지만, ③은 동사 뒤에 목적어(a strange noise)만 쓰인 구조이다.

10 give는 수여동사로 뒤에 「간접목적어(her)+직접목적어(some flowers)」 또는 「직접목적어(some flowers)+to+간접목적어(her)」 형태가 온다. for → to

11 '~한 냄새가 나다'는 「smell+형용사」로 나타낸다. beautifully → beautiful

12 lend는 수여동사로 뒤에 「간접목적어(him)+직접목적어(some money)」 또는 「직접목적어(some money)+to+간접목적어(him)」 형태가 온다.

13 '~을 …하게 만들다'는 「make+목적어+형용사」로 나타낸다.

14 send는 수여동사로 뒤에 「간접목적어(us)+직접목적어(a card)」 또는 「직접목적어(a card)+to+간접목적어(us)」 형태가 온다.

15 '~을 …라고 생각하다'는 「find+목적어(the work)+형용사(easy)」로 나타낸다.

Chapter 02 조동사

UNIT 01 Can / May

PRACTICE 1
p.30

1 can ride	**2** can't[cannot] open
3 Can, speak	**4** can't[cannot] go

해설
조동사 can은 '~할 수 있다'의 의미로, 능력이나 가능을 나타낸다. 부정문은 can't/cannot을 사용하고, 의문문은 can을 주어 앞으로 보내어 만든다.

PRACTICE 2
p.31

1 may go	**2** may not like
3 may use	**4** May, ask

해설
조동사 may는 '~일지도 모른다'라는 약한 추측과 '~해도 좋다'라는 허락의 의미를 나타낸다. 부정문은 may not을 사용하고, '~해도 좋습니까?'라고 상대방에게 허락을 구할 때는 'May I ~?'로 물을 수 있다.

문법 쏙쏙
pp.32~33

A

1 can	**2** can't	**3** can
4 can	**5** can	**6** can't
7 can	**8** can, can't	**9** can
10 can't	**11** Can	**12** can
13 can't	**14** can't	**15** can't

해설
1, 4, 5, 7, 8, 9, 12 ▸ '~할 수 있다'는 동사 앞에 can을 사용한다.
2, 6, 8, 10, 13, 14, 15 ▸ '~할 수 없다'는 동사 앞에 can't나 cannot을 사용한다.
3, 11 ▸ 상대방에게 어떤 것을 할 수 있는지를 물을 때는 can을 주어 앞으로 보내어 의문문을 만든다.

B

1 may be	**2** may not come
3 May, have	**4** may be
5 may use	**6** may not know
7 may rain	**8** May, see
9 may be	**10** may be
11 may leave	**12** may go
13 May, come	**14** may sell
15 may enter		

해설
1, 4, 7, 9, 10, 12, 14 ▸ '~일지도 모른다'라는 약한 추측은 동사 앞에 may를 사용한다.
2, 6 ▸ '~이 아닐지도 모른다'는 동사 앞에 may not을 사용한다.
5, 11, 15 ▸ '~해도 좋다'라는 허락의 의미는 동사 앞에 may를 사용한다.
3, 8, 13 ▸ '~해도 좋습니까?'라고 상대방에게 허락을 구할 때는 'May I ~?'로 물을 수 있다.

영작 술술
pp.34~35

A

1 I <u>can play</u> the violin.

2 <u>Can</u> you <u>make</u> a paper airplane?

3 My grandfather <u>can't[cannot]</u> <u>hear</u> well.

4 My dad <u>can drive</u> a truck.

5 When <u>can</u> you <u>finish</u> the work?

6 It <u>may be</u> true.

7 She <u>may know</u> the answer.

8 He <u>may not come</u> today.

9 <u>May</u> I <u>read</u> the newspaper?

10 You <u>may stay</u> here if you want to.

1 She can speak Chinese.

2 I can carry the box by myself.

3 Can you sing a song in English?

4 I can't[cannot] read these letters.

5 He may move next month.

6 You may not believe it.

7 I may go to Thailand this summer.

8 You may leave the hospital.

9 May I use the bathroom?

10 You may not park in this area.

WRAP UP

pp.36~37

A

1 can   **2** can't   **3** Can

4 may not   **5** may not   **6** use

7 I

해설

1 ▶ '~할 수 있다'는 동사 앞에 can을 사용한다.

2 ▶ '~할 수 없다'는 동사 앞에 can't/cannot을 사용한다.

3 ▶ 상대방에게 어떤 것을 할 수 있는지를 물을 때는 can을 주어 앞으로 보내어 의문문을 만든다. may는 상대방에게 허락을 구할 때 사용하며 의문문에서는 I, we만 주어로 사용할 수 있다.

4 ▶ '~이 아닐지도 모른다'라는 약한 추측은 동사 앞에 may not 을 사용한다.

5 ▶ '너무 춥다'라고 했으므로 '나가지 않을지도 모른다'라고 하는 것이 자연스럽다.

6 ▶ 조동사 may 뒤에는 동사원형이 온다.

7 ▶ may는 상대방에게 허락을 구할 때 사용하며 의문문에서는 I, we만 주어로 사용할 수 있다.

B

1 She can write English well.

2 You can't[cannot] run in the hallway.

3 Can you come to my house tomorrow?

4 He may become a doctor someday.

5 May I see your passport?

C   **1** ④   **2** ③

해설

1 ▶ ①, ②, ③은 '~일지도 모른다'라는 약한 추측, ④는 '~해도 좋다'라는 허락의 의미로 쓰였다.

2 ▶ 상대방에게 어떤 것을 할 수 있는지 묻는 표현이므로 'Can you ~?'로 시작해야 알맞다.

개념 Review

❶ 능력   ❷ 가능   ❸ 동사원형

❹ cannot   ❺ can't   ❻ 추측

❼ may not   ❽ May I

UNIT 02 Must / Have to

PRACTICE 1

p.38

1 must go   **2** must not be

3 must be   **4** must not know

해설

조동사 must는 '~해야 한다'라는 의무와 '~임에 틀림없다'라는 강한 추측의 의미를 나타낸다. 부정문은 must not/mustn't를 사용한다.

PRACTICE 2

p.39

1 has to   **2** has to

3 don't have to   **4** Do, have to

해설

have to는 '~해야 한다'라는 의미로 주어가 3인칭 단수(he/she/it)이면 has to로 바뀐다. 부정형은 don't/doesn't have to로 '~할 필요가 없다'를 의미하고, 의문문은 「Do/Does+주어+have to+동사원형 ~?」 형태이다.

문법 쏙쏙

pp.40~41

A

1 You have to wear your seatbelt.

2 She has to clean the bathroom.

3 You have to listen to your teacher.

4 He has to take out the garbage.

5 They have to pass the exam to graduate.

6 You have to stop at the red light.

7 We have to buy some milk.

8 I have to visit my friend in the hospital.

9 He has to do some exercise.

10 You have to fill out this form.

해설

must와 have to는 긍정문에서 모두 '~해야 한다'라는 의무의 뜻을 나타낸다. 단, 주어가 3인칭 단수(he/she/it)일 때 have to 는 has to로 써야 한다.

B

1 must	**2** don't have to
3 have to	**4** mustn't
5 have to	**6** must
7 must	**8** mustn't
9 mustn't	**10** doesn't have to
11 has to	**12** must
13 must not	**14** mustn't
15 have to	

해설

1, 5, 7, 11 > '~해야 한다'는 동사 앞에 must 또는 have to를 사용한다.

2, 10 > '~할 필요가 없다'는 동사 앞에 don't/doesn't have to를 사용한다.

3, 15 > '~해야 합니까?'는 「Do/Does+주어+have to+동사원형 ~?」으로 나타낸다.

4, 8, 9 > '~해서는 안 된다'는 동사 앞에 must not/mustn't를 사용한다.

6, 12, 13, 14 > '~임에/~가 아님에 틀림없다'라는 강한 추측은 조동사 must를 사용한다.

영작 술술
pp.42~43

A

1 I must tell him the truth.

2 You must stop eating junk food.

3 You must not smoke in here.

4 She must be a good friend.

5 They must not know the news.

6 All students have to wear school uniforms.

7 We don't have to hurry.

8 Does he have to leave now?

9 How long do I have to wait?

10 We have to brush our teeth three times a day.

B

1 I must[have to] wear glasses.

2 I must[have to] return the book.

3 You must not feed the animals.
[You mustn't feed the animals.]

4 You must not copy your friend's homework.
[You mustn't copy your friend's homework.]

5 It must be very exciting.

6 She must not feel well.[She mustn't feel well.]

7 Students must[have to] clean the classroom.

8 You don't have to worry.

9 Do we have to take the subway?

10 Does he have to work next weekend?

WRAP UP
pp.44~45

A

1 obey	**2** has to
3 must not	**4** must
5 must not	**6** don't have to
7 Do I have to	

해설

1 > must 뒤에는 동사원형이 온다. obeys → obey

2 > 주어가 3인칭 단수(he)이므로 have to를 has to로 바꿔야 한다.

3, 5 > '~해서는 안 된다'는 「must not/mustn't+동사원형」으로 나타낸다.

4 > '~임에 틀림없다'는 must를 사용한다.

6 > '~할 필요가 없다'는 don't/doesn't have to를 사용한다.

7 > '~해야 합니까?'는 「Do/Does+주어+have to+동사원형 ~?」 형태이다. must로는 의문문을 만들 수 없다.

B

1 You must[have to] get some rest.

2 You must not walk on the grass.

3 He must like action movies.

4 You don't have to buy a ticket.

5 How long do we have to wait for the bus?

C

1 ④	**2** ④

해설

1 > ①, ②, ③은 의무(~해야 한다), ④는 강한 추측(~임에 틀림없다)을 나타낸다.

2 > '~할 필요가 없다'는 don't/doesn't have to를 사용한다.

개념 Review

❶ 의무	**❷** 금지	**❸** 강한 추측
❹ mustn't	**❺** 의무	**❻** 동사원형

ACTUAL TEST
pp.46~47

01 ①	**02** ④	**03** ③	**04** ③
05 ③	**06** Do, have to		
07 can see	**08** ④	**09** ②	**10** ③
11 ②	**12** ②	**13** ③	

14 You must not be late again.
[You mustn't be late again.]

15 Mike doesn't have to go to the dentist.

01 '~일지도 모른다'라는 약한 추측은 동사 앞에 may를 사용한다.

02 비가 오지 않는다고 했으므로 '우산을 가져갈 필요가 없다'라는 뜻이 되어야 자연스럽다.

03 must(~해야 한다)와 바꿔 쓸 수 있는 것은 have to이다.

04 may와 must는 추측, has to는 의무를 나타낸다.

05 첫 번째 빈칸에는 can't, have to, must 등이 가능하지만, 두 번째 빈칸에는 금지를 뜻하는 mustn't가 알맞다.

06 '~해야 합니까?'는 「Do/Does+주어+have to+동사원형 ~?」 형태로 나타낸다.

07 '~할 수 있다'는 can을 사용한다.

08 ①, ②, ③은 약한 추측(~일지도 모른다), ④는 허락(~해도 좋습니까?)을 나타낸다.

09 ①, ③, ④는 금지(~해서는 안 된다), ②는 강한 추측(~임에 틀림없다)을 나타낸다.

10 May I open the door? 또는 Can you open the door?로 고쳐야 자연스럽다.

11 must 뒤에는 동사원형이 온다. must to do → must do

12 '~이 아닐지도 모른다'는 may not을 사용한다.

13 '~임에 틀림없다'는 must를 사용한다.

14 '~해서는 안 된다'는 must not/mustn't를 사용한다.

15 '~할 필요가 없다'는 don't/doesn't have to를 사용한다.

Chapter **03** 비교

UNIT **01** 비교급과 최상급: 규칙 변화

PRACTICE **1** p.50

1 slower, slowest
2 hotter, hottest
3 prettier, prettiest
4 more important, most important

해설

1 ▸ 대부분의 형용사/부사의 비교급과 최상급은 -er, -est를 붙여 만들고, -e로 끝나면 -r, -st만 붙인다.
2 ▸ 「단모음+단자음」으로 끝나면 마지막 자음을 한번 더 쓰고 -er, -est를 붙인다.
3 ▸ -y로 끝나면 y를 i로 고치고 -er, -est를 붙인다.
4 ▸ 2음절 이상이면 more, most를 붙인다.

PRACTICE **2** p.51

1 sweeter   2 hottest
3 more beautiful   4 most expensive

해설

1, 3 ▸ '~보다'를 뜻하는 than 앞에는 비교급이 와야 한다.
2, 4 ▸ 정관사 the 뒤에는 최상급이 와야 한다.

문법 쏙쏙 pp.52~53

A

1 older, oldest
2 shorter, shortest
3 bigger, biggest
4 faster, fastest
5 larger, largest
6 hotter, hottest
7 cheaper, cheapest
8 easier, easiest
9 wider, widest
10 colder, coldest
11 heavier, heaviest
12 thinner, thinnest
13 more useful, most useful
14 more expensive, most expensive
15 more attractive, most attractive

해설

1, 2, 4, 7, 10 ▸ 대부분의 형용사/부사의 비교급과 최상급은 -er, -est를 붙여 만든다.
3, 6, 12 ▸ 「단모음+단자음」으로 끝나면 마지막 자음을 한번 더 쓰고 -er, -est를 붙인다.
5, 9 ▸ -e로 끝나면 -r, -st만 붙인다.
8, 11 ▸ -y로 끝나면 y를 i로 고치고 -er, -est를 붙인다.
13, 14, 15 ▸ 2음절 이상이면 more, most를 붙인다.

B

1 bigger   2 nicer
3 tallest   4 higher
5 luckiest   6 faster
7 hotter   8 healthier
9 shortest   10 cheaper
11 prettiest   12 oldest
13 busier   14 most interesting
15 more intelligent

해설

1 ▸ 최상급 앞에는 정관사 the가 와야 하므로, '더 큰'을 의미하는 비교급 bigger가 알맞다.

2, 4, 6, 7, 8, 10, 13, 15 ▶ '~보다'를 뜻하는 than 앞에는 비교급이 와야 한다.

3, 5, 9, 11, 12, 14 ▶ 정관사 the 뒤에는 최상급이 와야 한다.

영작 술술

pp.54~55

A

1 Jimmy is lazier than Tom.

2 I got up earlier than usual.

3 Roses are more beautiful than tulips.

4 The necklace is more expensive than the bracelet.

5 Jane got the highest score on the test.

6 January is the coldest month of the year.

7 I am the youngest person in my family.

8 This is the oldest building in the neighborhood.

9 Soccer is the most popular sport in Italy.

10 This is the tallest tree in the park.

B

1 Mt. Baekdu is higher than Mt. Halla.

2 Today is warmer than yesterday.

3 Tina is thinner than her sister.

4 Good health is more important than money.

5 Chinese is more difficult than English.

6 Today is the saddest day of my life.

7 The Nile is the longest river in the world.

8 Seoul is the largest city in Korea.

9 He is the most handsome boy in the class.

10 Bach is the greatest musician in history.

WRAP UP

pp.56~57

A

1 easier **2** cleaner

3 hottest **4** older

5 fastest **6** wisest

7 the longest hotdog

해설

1 ▶ -y로 끝나면 y를 i로 고치고 -er, -est를 붙인다. easyer → easier

2 ▶ clean의 비교급은 cleaner이다.

3 ▶ hot은 「단모음(o)+단자음(t)」으로 끝나므로 마지막 자음을 하나 더 쓰고 -est를 붙인다. hotest → hottest

4 ▶ '~보다'를 뜻하는 than 앞에는 비교급이 와야 한다. oldest → older

5 ▶ fast의 최상급은 fastest이다.

6 ▶ 정관사 the 뒤에는 최상급이 와야 한다. wiser → wisest

7 ▶ '세상에서 가장 긴 핫도그'라는 의미의 최상급 표현이므로 a를 the로 고쳐야 알맞다.

B

1 Bicycles are safer than motorcycles.

2 John is fatter than Mike.

3 The country is more peaceful than the city.

4 Amy is the shortest girl in the class.

5 My diary is the most important thing to me.

C **1** ① **2** ②

해설

1 ▶ big은 「단모음(i)+단자음(g)」으로 끝나므로 마지막 자음을 하나 더 쓰고 -er, -est를 붙인다. big – bigger – biggest

2 ▶ '~보다 더 …한'은 「비교급(brighter)+than」 구문을 사용한다.

개념 Review

❶ -er **❷** more **❸** -est

❹ most **❺** 비교급 **❻** 최상급

UNIT **02** 비교급과 최상급: 불규칙 변화

PRACTICE **1**

p.58

1 better, best **2** worse, worst

3 more, most **4** less, least

해설

일부 형용사와 부사들은 비교급과 최상급이 불규칙하게 변화하므로 주의해야 한다.

PRACTICE **2**

p.59

1 better and better **2** much

3 richest **4** more and more

해설

1, 4 ▶ '점점 더 ~한'은 「비교급+and+비교급」으로 나타낸다.

2 ▶ '훨씬 더 ~한'은 「much+비교급」으로 나타낸다.

3 ▶ '가장 ~한 … 중의 하나'는 「one of the+최상급+복수 명사」로 나타낸다.

A

1 good	2 more	3 worst
4 less	5 better	6 better
7 little	8 worse	9 best
10 less	11 least	12 better
13 bad	14 least	15 most

해설

1, 7, 13 ▸ 비교의 대상 없이 단순 사실을 말할 경우에는 원급을 쓴다.

2, 4, 5, 6, 10, 12 ▸ '~보다'를 뜻하는 than 앞에는 비교급이 와야 한다.

3, 9, 11, 14, 15 ▸ 정관사 the 뒤에는 최상급이 와야 한다.

8 ▸ '내 필체보다 Tara의 것이 더 안 좋다'라는 비교를 의미를 담고 있으므로 비교급 worse가 알맞다.

B

1 I feel much better than yesterday.
2 My grandfather is much older than me.
3 Your room is much cleaner than mine.
4 Gold is much more expensive than silver.
5 The balloon is getting bigger and bigger.
6 The game got more and more exciting.
7 More and more people are buying electric cars.
8 The film is one of the best movies of the year.
9 It is one of the largest cities in the country.
10 Arabic is one of the most difficult languages.

해설

1-4 ▸ '훨씬 더 ~한'은 「much+비교급」으로 나타낸다.

5-7 ▸ '점점 더 ~한'은 「비교급+and+비교급」으로 나타낸다.

8-10 ▸ '가장 ~한 … 중의 하나'는 「one of the+최상급+복수명사」로 나타낸다.

영작 술술

A

1 Sarah has <u>more books than</u> Kelly.
2 I like Korean food <u>more[better] than</u> Western food.
3 Who is <u>the best teacher</u> at your school?
4 It was <u>the worst day</u> of my life.
5 Those are <u>the least expensive</u> shoes in the shop.
6 China has <u>the most people</u> in the world.

7 His new car is <u>much faster than</u> his old one.
8 This movie is <u>much more</u> interesting than the book.
9 The hole in my sock is getting <u>bigger and bigger</u>.
10 It is <u>one of the most popular</u> menu items at the restaurant.

B

1 David is a better player than Ryan.
2 Ann got the best grade in the class.
3 He is the worst singer of the three.
4 Sally is much more outgoing than her sister.
5 My allowance is less than 20 dollars a week.
6 I went to bed much later than usual.
7 He is the least popular student in the class.
8 Her health is getting worse and worse.
9 He became more and more famous.
10 It was one of the most impressive speeches.

WRAP UP

A

1 best	2 better
3 worst	4 more
5 much nicer	6 thinner and thinner
7 the funniest movies	

해설

1 ▸ '노래를 가장 잘하는 사람'이라는 의미가 되어야 하므로 good의 최상급인 best가 와야 한다.

2 ▸ '~보다'를 뜻하는 than 앞에는 비교급이 와야 한다.
good → better

3 ▸ '옷을 가장 잘 못 입는 사람'이라는 의미가 되어야 하므로 bad의 최상급인 worst가 와야 한다. worse → worst

4 ▸ '~보다'를 뜻하는 than 앞에는 비교급이 와야 한다.
most → more

5 ▸ '훨씬 더 ~한'은 「much+비교급」으로 나타낸다.
much nice → much nicer

6 ▸ '점점 더 ~한'은 「비교급+and+비교급」으로 나타낸다.
thin and thin → thinner and thinner

7 ▸ '가장 ~한 … 중의 하나'는 「one of the+최상급+복수명사」로 나타낸다. the funniest movie → the funniest movies

B

1 She is less friendly than her sister.
2 I got the worst grade in the class.

3 His house is much bigger than ours.

4 The weather is getting colder and colder.

5 The book is one of the best sellers.

C   **1** ③   **2** ③

해설

1 ▸ '가장 덜 비싼'은 the least expensive이다.

2 ▸ '가장 ~한 … 중의 하나'는 「one of the＋최상급＋복수 명사」로 나타낸다.

개념 Review

① much   **②** 비교급   **③** 비교급
④ 최상급   **⑤** 복수 명사

ACTUAL TEST
pp.66~67

01 ④   **02** ③   **03** ②   **04** ①

05 ②   **06** more[better] than

07 More and more   **08** ②   **09** ③

10 ②   **11** ②   **12** ①   **13** ③

14 Sunflowers are bigger than roses.

15 He is one of the most famous actors in the world.

01 than 앞에는 비교급인 more interesting이 와야 한다.

02 '가장 ~한 … 중의 하나'는 「one of the＋최상급＋복수 명사」로 나타낸다.

03 little은 불규칙 변화를 하는 형용사이자 부사로 little – less – least가 알맞다.

04 '훨씬 더 ~한'은 「much＋비교급」으로 나타낸다.

05 '내 인생에서 가장 ~한 날'의 의미가 되어야 하므로 비교급 인 worse는 올 수 없다.

06 'B보다 A를 더 좋아하다'는 「like A more[better] than B」로 나타낸다.

07 '점점 더 많은'은 「비교급＋and＋비교급」 구문을 사용해 more and more로 나타낸다.

08 'Tom이 Jack보다 더 크다'라는 뜻의 비교 구문이 와야 하 므로 taller than이 알맞다.

09 than 앞에는 비교급인 smarter가 와야 한다.

10 「one of the＋최상급＋복수 명사」이므로 musical의 복수형 musicals가 알맞다.

11 ① the worst dancer ③ warmer ④ less로 고쳐야 한다.

12 '더 많은 신발'은 more pairs of shoes이다.

13 '점점 더 ~한'이라는 뜻의 「비교급＋and＋비교급」 구문을 사용해 fatter and fatter로 나타낸다.

14 '~보다 더 …한'은 「비교급＋than」으로 나타낸다.

15 '가장 ~한 … 중의 하나'는 「one of the＋최상급＋복수 명사」로 나타낸다.

Chapter 04 전치사

UNIT 01 시간의 전치사

PRACTICE 1
p.70

1. in   **2.** at   **3.** on   **4.** in
5. in   **6.** in   **7.** on   **8.** at

해설

at은 구체적인 시각, 특정한 시점, in은 연도, 월, 계절 등 비교적 긴 시간, on은 요일, 날짜, 특정한 날 앞에 사용한다.

PRACTICE 2
p.71

1 after   **2** from, to
3 until   **4** for

해설

after는 '~ 후에', from ~ to...는 '~부터 …까지', until은 '~까지'를 나타내며, for는 '~ 동안'의 의미로 뒤에 기간을 나타내는 숫자가 온다.

문법 쏙쏙
pp.72~73

A

1 in   **2** at   **3** on
4 in   **5** at   **6** in
7 in   **8** on   **9** at
10 in   **11** on   **12** in
13 on   **14** in   **15** on

해설

1, 4, 7, 10, 14 ▸ 연도, 월, 계절 등 비교적 긴 시간 앞에는 in을 사용한다.

6, 9, 12 ▸ '아침에/점심에/저녁에'는 in the morning/in the afternoon/in the evening이지만, '정오에/밤에/자정에'는 at noon/at night/at midnight이다.

2, 5 ▸ 구체적인 시각 앞에는 at을 사용한다.

3, 8, 15 ▸ 요일, 날짜, 특정한 날 앞에는 on을 사용한다.

11 ▸ '주말에'는 on the weekend이다.

13 ▸ 특정 요일의 아침/점심/저녁 앞에는 on을 사용한다.

B

1 for   **2** after   **3** during
4 to   **5** for   **6** before
7 for   **8** during   **9** until

10 after	**11** for	**12** during
13 until	**14** from	**15** during

해설
1, 5, 7, 11 ▷ '~ 동안'의 의미로 기간을 나타내는 숫자 앞에는 for를 사용한다.
2, 10 ▷ '~ 후에'는 after를 사용한다.
3, 8, 12, 15 ▷ '~ 동안'의 의미로 특정 기간을 나타내는 명사 앞에는 during을 사용한다.
4, 14 ▷ '~부터 …까지'는 from ~ to...를 사용한다.
6 ▷ '~ 전에'는 before를 사용한다.
9, 13 ▷ '~까지'는 until을 사용한다.

영작 술술

pp.74~75

Ⓐ

1 The building was built in 2019.
2 Let's meet at 1 o'clock on Saturday.
3 She often goes shopping on the weekend.
4 I always take a walk after lunch.
5 They talked on the phone until 10 o'clock.
6 He arrived at school before 9 o'clock.
7 We work during the day and sleep at night.
8 We took a break for 10 minutes.
9 The art museum is open from Monday to Friday.
10 You cannot talk loudly during class.

Ⓑ

1 The class finished at 2:30.
2 Many people visit Canada in fall.
3 I had dinner with my family on my birthday.
4 She worked there for five years.
5 He has to work during the summer holiday.
6 They had lunch before the meeting.
7 Ann went to the library after school.
8 We have class from 9:00 a.m. to 4:00 p.m.
9 He waited for me until 6 o'clock.
10 My parents got married on July 10, 2010.

WRAP UP

pp.76~77

Ⓐ

1 on	**2** in	**3** in	**4** at
5 on	**6** for	**7** from	

해설
1 ▷ 날짜 앞에는 on을 사용한다.
2, 3 ▷ 월, 연도 앞에는 in을 사용한다.
4 ▷ '정오에/밤에/자정에'는 at noon/at night/at midnight 이다.
5 ▷ 특정 요일의 아침/점심/저녁 앞에는 on을 사용한다.
6 ▷ 기간을 나타내는 숫자(eight hours) 앞에는 for를 사용한다.
7 ▷ '~부터 …까지'는 from ~ to...를 사용한다.

Ⓑ

1 He left work at 10 o'clock.
2 I usually take a nap after lunch.
3 He studied abroad for six years.
4 I visited my grandparents on New Year's Day.
5 The buses run until midnight.

Ⓒ
1 ②		**2** ④	

해설
1 ▷ '자정에'는 at midnight이다.
2 ▷ '밤에'는 at night이고, '~ 동안'의 의미로 특정 기간을 나타내는 명사 앞에는 during을 사용한다.

개념 Review

❶ 시간		❷ 장소		❸ at	
❹ in		❺ on		❻ for	
❼ during					

UNIT **02** 장소의 전치사

PRACTICE **1**

p.78

1 on	**2** in
3 next to	**4** under

해설
'~ 안에' 또는 마을, 도시, 국가 등 비교적 넓은 장소 앞에는 in, '~ 위에'는 on, '~ 아래에'는 under, '~ 옆에'는 next to를 사용한다.

PRACTICE **2**

p.79

1 across from	**2** behind
3 in front of	**4** between

해설
'~ 앞에'는 in front of, '~ 뒤에'는 behind, '~ 사이에'는 between, '~ 맞은편에'는 across from을 사용한다.

문법 쏙쏙

pp.80~81

A

1 in	**2** on	**3** under
4 on	**5** in	**6** between
7 next to	**8** in front of	

해설

1, 5 > '~ 안에'는 in을 사용한다.

2, 4 > 수평면이 아니더라도 표면에 맞닿아 있으면 on(~ 위에)을 사용한다.

3 > '~ 아래에'는 under를 사용한다.

6 > '~ 사이에'는 between을 사용한다.

7 > '~ 옆에'는 next to를 사용한다.

8 > '~ 앞에'는 in front of를 사용한다.

B

1 in	**2** in	
3 on	**4** on	
5 next to	**6** behind	
7 under	**8** in front of	
9 on	**10** between	
11 on	**12** in	
13 between	**14** on	
15 across from		

해설

1, 2, 12 > '~ 안에' 또는 마을, 도시, 국가 등 비교적 넓은 장소 앞에는 in을 사용한다.

3, 4, 9, 11, 14 > 어떤 것의 표면 '위에'는 전치사 on을 사용한다.

5 > between 뒤에는 복수 명사나 A and B 형태가 와야 하므로 적절하지 않다.

6 > '문 뒤에'를 뜻하는 behind the door가 적절하다.

7 > '나무 아래에'를 뜻하는 under the tree가 적절하다.

8 > '학교 앞에서'를 뜻하는 in front of the school이 적절하다.

10, 13 > 복수 명사나 A and B 형태 앞에는 '~ 사이에'를 뜻하는 between이 적절하다.

15 > '은행 맞은편에'를 뜻하는 across from the bank가 적절하다.

영작 술술

pp.82~83

A

1 He is studying in his room.

2 People are swimming in the sea.

3 He parked his car in front of the building.

4 The boy hid behind the door.

5 I found my cell phone under the bed.

6 She put some lotion on her face.

7 They are sitting across from each other.

8 I sat between Jack and Cindy.

9 Who is the man next to the window?

10 She has a small garden behind her house.

B

1 There are a lot of fish in the aquarium.

2 There is a stain on his shirt.

3 She put the apples in the basket.

4 Dave is sitting between Jane and Mina.

5 The girl is standing next to the tree.

6 The bus stops in front of the hotel.

7 The hospital is across from the hair salon.

8 They are relaxing under the beach umbrella.

9 I dropped my pencil behind the desk.

10 The bookstore is next to the post office.

WRAP UP

pp.84~85

A

1 on	**2** in	**3** on
4 next to	**5** behind	**6** in front of
7 and		

해설

1 > '접시 위에'는 on the plate이다.

2 > '내 주머니 안에'는 in my pocket이다.

3 > '바닥 위에'는 on the floor이다.

4 > '~ 옆에'는 next to를 사용한다.

5 > '~ 뒤에'는 behind를 사용한다.

6 > '~ 앞에'는 in front of를 사용한다.

7 > 'A와 B 사이에'는 between A and B로 나타낸다.

B

1 She is cooking in the kitchen.

2 There are three cushions on the sofa.

3 He is reading a book under the tree.

4 The taxi stand is next to the bus stop.

5 The police station is across from the fire station.

C   **1** ④   **2** ④

해설

1 > ①, ②, ③은 '~ 안에'를 의미하는 in, ④는 얼굴 표면 위를 가리켜야 하므로 on이 알맞다.

2 > Vine Street and Main Street 앞에는 between(~ 사이에)이 와야 하고, from 앞에는 across from(~ 맞은편에)의 across가 와야 한다.

① 장소　　　**② 위치**　　　**③ 복수 명사**

ACTUAL TEST
pp.86~87

01 ③	**02** ①	**03** ③	**04** ②
05 ④	**06** from, to		
07 across from		**08** ②	**09** ④
10 ④	**11** ②	**12** ②	**13** ①

14 He hurt his leg during the soccer game.
15 The bank is between the café and the bakery.

01 날짜 앞에는 on을 사용한다.
02 마을, 도시, 국가 등 비교적 넓은 장소 앞에는 in을 사용한다.
03 '12시까지 자지 않았다'는 until(~까지)을 사용하고, in과 of 사이에는 in front of(~ 앞에)의 front가 와야 한다.
04 ①, ③, ④는 on, ② '자정에'는 at midnight이다.
05 ①, ②, ③은 in, ④ '바닥에'는 on the floor이다.
06 '~부터 …까지'는 from ~ to…를 사용한다.
07 '~ 맞은편에'는 across from을 사용한다.
08 '~ 위에'를 뜻하는 on은 적절하지 않다.
09 between 뒤에는 복수 명사나 A and B 형태가 와야 하므로 적절하지 않다.
10 기간을 나타내는 숫자(two hours) 앞에는 for를 사용한다.
11 '벽에'는 on the wall이다.
12 구체적인 시각 앞에는 at을 사용한다.
13 '~ 뒤에'를 뜻하는 전치사는 behind이다.
14 '축구 시합 중에'는 during the soccer game이다.
15 '카페와 빵집 사이에'는 between the café and the bakery이다.

Chapter 05 접속사

UNIT 01 등위 접속사

PRACTICE 1
p.90

1 shiny	**2** fun
3 on foot	**4** pears

해설
등위 접속사 and는 서로 비슷한 내용을, but은 서로 반대되는

내용을 연결할 때 사용하고, or는 둘 중 하나를 가리키는 경우에 사용한다.

PRACTICE 2
p.91

1 I had dinner.
2 I took some medicine.
3 he bought a new one.
4 do you want to go?

해설
등위 접속사 and는 서로 비슷한 내용을, but은 서로 반대되는 내용을 연결할 때 사용하고, or는 둘 중 하나를 가리키는 경우에 사용한다. so는 '그래서'라는 뜻으로 원인과 결과를 나타내는 절을 연결할 때 사용한다.

문법 쏙쏙
pp.92~93

A

1 and	**2** but	**3** or
4 and	**5** or	**6** and
7 but	**8** or	**9** and
10 or	**11** and	**12** so
13 but	**14** or	**15** but

해설
1, 4, 6, 9, 11 ▷ 서로 비슷하거나 이어지는 내용은 and(~와, 그리고)로 연결한다.
2, 7, 13, 15 ▷ 서로 반대되는 내용은 but(~지만, 그러나)으로 연결한다.
3, 5, 8, 10, 14 ▷ 둘 중 하나를 가리키는 경우는 or(~거나, 또는)로 연결한다.
12 ▷ 원인과 결과는 so(그래서)로 연결한다.

B

1 I am 14 years old, and my sister is 12 years old.
2 It is a great house, but it doesn't have a yard.
3 We can eat out, or we can eat at home.
4 It was cold, so I turned on the heater.
5 My little brother can read, but he can't write.
6 The bus stopped, and a woman got off.
7 The movie was boring, so I fell asleep.
8 Tom gave his girlfriend a present, and she loved it.
9 You can fix your bike, or you can buy a new one.
10 You can walk to the station, but it's a little far.

1, 6, 8 ▶ 서로 비슷하거나 이어지는 내용은 and(~와, 그리고)로 연결한다.

2, 5, 10 ▶ 서로 반대되는 내용은 but(~지만, 그러나)으로 연결한다.

3, 9 ▶ 둘 중 하나를 가리키는 경우는 or(~거나, 또는)로 연결한다.

4, 7 ▶ 원인과 결과는 so(그래서)로 연결한다.

영작 술술
pp.94~95

A

1 Green and yellow are my favorite colors.

2 The book was boring but useful.

3 Will you clean or cook?

4 We went to the market and bought some food.

5 She was cold, so she put on her coat.

6 I can sing, but I can't[cannot] dance.

7 Do you want to watch TV or listen to music?

8 He played the guitar, and I played the keyboard.

9 Tom washed his hands, but he didn't wash his face.

10 I have to work, so I can't[cannot] go to Sam's party.

B

1 The room is clean and tidy.

2 Is the answer right or wrong?

3 She is smart but forgetful.

4 She went home and got some rest.

5 I know his face, but I don't know his name.

6 We can go to the park, or we can stay at home.

7 It was dark, so I turned on the light.

8 The food was delicious, and the service was excellent.

9 He needed some money, so he got a part-time job.

10 I wanted to go out, but it started raining.

WRAP UP
pp.96~97

A

1 or	**2** and	**3** but
4 or	**5** and	**6** so
7 but		

1 ▶ '수프로 하시겠어요 샐러드로 하시겠어요?'의 의미이므로 and → or

2 ▶ '귀걸이와 목걸이를 착용하고 있다'의 의미이므로 but → and

3 ▶ '열심히 노력했지만 경기에 졌다'의 의미이므로 or → but

4 ▶ '버스로 가거나 걸어갈 수 있다'의 의미이므로 so → or

5 ▶ '책을 읽었는데 좋아했다'의 의미이므로 but → and

6 ▶ '돈이 없어서 쇼핑하러 갈 수 없다'의 의미이므로 but → so

7 ▶ '축구하는 것을 좋아하지만 잘은 못한다'의 의미이므로 so → but

B

1 Bears and snakes are dangerous animals.

2 He will move to New York or L.A.

3 She eats fish, but she doesn't eat meat.

4 It rained a lot, so we didn't go out.

5 I have a Spanish friend, and her name is Luisa.

C 1 ④ 2 ②

1 ▶ '그의 생일이었지만 그는 나를 초대하지 않았다'의 의미이므로 so → but

2 ▶ 첫 번째 문장은 '바다에서 살지만 물고기가 아니다'의 의미이므로 but, 두 번째 문장은 '내일 시험이 있어서 오늘 밤 공부해야 한다'의 의미이므로 so가 알맞다.

개념 Review

❶ 등위 접속사	❷ and	❸ but
❹ or	❺ 콤마(,)	❻ so

UNIT 02 종속 접속사

PRACTICE 1
p.98

1 when I first met him.

2 after we had dinner.

3 when she got married.

4 before he left home.

종속 접속사 when은 '~할 때', before는 '~ 전에', after는 '~ 후에'를 의미한다.

1 because	**2** If
3 because	**4** if

해설

종속 접속사 because는 '~ 때문에'라는 의미로 이유를 나타낼 때, if는 '(만약) ~하다면'이라는 의미로 조건을 나타낼 때 사용한다.

문법 쏙쏙   pp.100~101

A

1 when the alarm clock rang
2 before she went to Paris
3 after he woke up
4 if you turn left
5 because it is a holiday
6 before the movie started
7 when I grow up
8 after he ran the marathon
9 if you don't have a map
10 because he hurt his leg

해설

1, 7 ▷ when은 '~ 할 때'를 의미한다.
2, 6 ▷ before는 '~ 전에'를 의미한다.
3, 8 ▷ after는 '~ 후에'를 의미한다.
4, 9 ▷ if는 '(만약) ~하다면'이라는 뜻으로 조건을 나타낸다.
5, 10 ▷ because는 '~ 때문에'라는 뜻으로 이유를 나타낸다.

B

1 I turned on the air conditioner because it was hot.
2 If I drink too much coffee, I can't sleep at night.
3 I must go to the bank before it closes.
4 When she went out, she locked the door.
5 Jean hung out the clothes to dry after she washed them.
6 If it snows, I will make a snowman.
7 I always wash my hands before I eat food.
8 I don't like big cities because they are too crowded.
9 I will buy the car if the price goes down.
10 When I was a child, I didn't eat spinach.

해설

1 ▷ '더웠기 때문에 에어컨을 켰다'라고 해야 자연스럽다.
2 ▷ '커피를 너무 많이 마시면 잠을 잘 수 없다'라고 해야 자연스럽다.
3 ▷ '문을 닫기 전에 가야 한다'라고 해야 자연스럽다.
4 ▷ '나갈 때 문을 잠갔다'라고 해야 자연스럽다.
5 ▷ '옷을 세탁한 후 널었다'라고 해야 자연스럽다.
6 ▷ '눈이 온다면 눈사람을 만들 것이다'라고 해야 자연스럽다.
7 ▷ '음식을 먹기 전에 손을 씻는다'라고 해야 자연스럽다.
8 ▷ '너무 복잡하기 때문에 대도시를 좋아하지 않는다'라고 해야 자연스럽다.
9 ▷ '가격이 내려가면 그 차를 살 것이다'라고 해야 자연스럽다.
10 ▷ '아이였을 때 시금치를 먹지 않았다'라고 해야 자연스럽다.

영작 술술   pp.102~103

A

1 When the weather is hot, I drink a lot of water.
2 He looked both ways before he crossed the street.
3 If you exercise regularly, you will be healthier.
4 She went to bed after she finished her homework.
5 He didn't come to school because he was sick.
6 I took my umbrella before I left home.
7 He was full because he ate[had] two hamburgers.
8 When I was in trouble, he helped me.
9 After she brushes her teeth, she doesn't eat any snacks.
10 If you wake[get] up late, you will be late for school.

B

1 When I am home, I usually watch TV.
2 He watered the flowers before he left.
3 I passed the exam because I studied hard.
4 If you don't hurry, you will miss the bus.
5 He felt refreshed after he took a shower.
6 When she saw me, she waved at me.
7 He booked a hotel room before he went to Tokyo.
8 I went to the concert because I liked the singer.
9 If we take the subway, we will get there faster.
10 He laughed when he heard the funny joke.

WRAP UP

A

1 d	**2** a	**3** e	**4** f
5 g	**6** b	**7** c	

해설

1 ▸ '더웠기 때문에 코트를 벗었다'라고 해야 자연스럽다.

2 ▸ '단것을 너무 많이 먹으면 뚱뚱해질 것이다'라고 해야 자연스럽다.

3 ▸ '집에 도착했을 때 그곳에 아무도 없었다'라고 해야 자연스럽다.

4 ▸ '너무 늦기 전에 집에 가야 한다'라고 해야 자연스럽다.

5 ▸ '고등학교를 마친 후 대학에 갔다'라고 해야 자연스럽다.

6 ▸ '식사하기 전에 항상 기도한다'라고 해야 자연스럽다.

7 ▸ '여권이 없으면 해외여행을 할 수 없다'라고 해야 자연스럽다.

B

1 After she sat at the desk, she opened her textbook.

2 I met Jane when I was in New York.

3 Because the class was boring, I fell asleep.

4 I cleaned the house before my parents came home.

5 If you exercise every day, you will lose weight.

C **1** ④　　　　**2** ③

해설

1 ▸ '친절하기 때문에' 좋아하는 것이므로 because가 알맞다.

2 ▸ 조건을 뜻하는 if가 이끄는 절에는 미래 시제를 사용하지 않으므로 첫 번째 빈칸은 현재 시제인 rains가, 두 번째 빈칸은 '취소할 것이다'의 의미인 미래 시제 will cancel이 알맞다.

개념 Review

❶ when	❷ before	❸ after
❹ 콤마(,)	❺ 현재 시제	

ACTUAL TEST

01 ③	**02** ④	**03** ①	**04** ③
05 ③	**06** If, don't drive		
07 when, was		**08** ③	**09** ④
10 ①	**11** ④	**12** ②	**13** ①

14 He is rich, but he doesn't spend much money.

15 If you don't eat now, you will be hungry later.

01 둘 중 하나를 가리키는 경우는 or을 사용한다.

02 '몸이 좋지 않기 때문에' 집에 있었으므로 because가 알맞다.

03 'Bill은 기타를 갖고 있는데, 그것을 매우 잘 친다'의 의미로, 서로 비슷하거나 이어지는 내용은 and로 연결한다.

04 '쿠키를 구운 후' 나에게 준 것이므로 after가 알맞다.

05 첫 번째 빈칸은 '도울 수 있으니 걱정할 필요 없다'의 의미이므로 so가 알맞고, 두 번째 빈칸은 '자기 전에' 우유를 마신 것이므로 before가 와야 한다.

06 '(만약) ~하다면'은 종속 접속사 if를 사용한다.

07 '~할 때'는 종속 접속사 when을 사용하고, 과거 시제이므로 동사는 was를 사용한다.

08 '그를 방문했지만 그는 마을에 없었다'의 의미이므로 so → but

09 '더 빨리 걷는다면 기차를 탈 것이다'의 의미이므로 Before → If

10 조건을 뜻하는 if가 이끄는 절에는 미래 시제 대신 현재 시제를 사용하므로 will be → am

11 ①, ②, ③은 but, ④는 and가 알맞다.

12 원인과 결과를 연결할 때는 so나 because를 사용한다. ④는 원인과 결과가 서로 바뀌어 알맞지 않다.

13 '연극이 끝나기 전에'는 before the play ended이다.

14 서로 반대되는 내용은 but(~지만, 그러나)으로 연결한다.

15 '(만약) ~하다면'은 종속 접속사 if를 사용한다.

Chapter 06 감탄문과 명령문

UNIT 01 감탄문

PRACTICE 1　　　　　　　　　　p.110

1 What a rude man he is!

2 What kind people they are!

3 What beautiful eyes she has!

4 What a stupid mistake I made!

해설

What으로 시작하는 감탄문은 「What(+a/an)+형용사+명사+주어+동사」의 어순이다. 명사가 복수이거나 셀 수 없는 명사일 경우 a/an은 쓰지 않는다.

1 How slowly the boy is eating!
2 How heavy this shopping bag is!
3 How beautifully she paints!
4 How well you play the guitar!

(해설)

How로 시작하는 감탄문은 「How+형용사/부사+주어+동사!」
의 어순이다.

문법 쏙쏙
pp.112~113

A

1 How	**2** What	**3** How
4 What	**5** How	**6** What
7 How	**8** How	**9** What
10 How	**11** How	**12** What
13 How	**14** What	**15** What

(해설)

1, 3, 5, 7, 8, 10, 11, 13 ▶ 뒤에 「형용사/부사+주어+동사」가
이어지므로 How가 알맞다.
2, 4, 6, 12, 15 ▶ 뒤에 「a/an+형용사+명사」가 이어지므로
What이 알맞다.
9 ▶ 뒤에 「형용사+명사」가 이어지므로 What이 알맞다.
children이 복수이므로 a는 쓰이지 않았다.
14 ▶ 뒤에 「형용사+명사」가 이어지므로 What이 알맞다.
weather는 셀 수 없는 명사이므로 a는 쓰이지 않았다.

B

1 What a high mountain it is!
2 How clever your daughter is!
3 What a good cook he is!
4 How cheap these jeans are!
5 How tired I am!
6 What long legs she has!
7 How badly he dances!
8 What a big mistake I made!
9 How quickly the rabbit ran away!
10 What a nice jacket you are wearing!

(해설)

1, 3, 6, 8, 10 ▶ 명사구를 강조하는 감탄문은 What으로 시작하고
「What(+a/an)+형용사+명사+주어+동사!」의 어순이다.
2, 4, 5, 7, 9 ▶ 형용사나 부사를 강조하는 감탄문은 How로 시작
하고 「How+형용사/부사+주어+동사!」의 어순이다.

영작 술술
pp.114~115

A

1 What a lazy boy he is!
2 How beautiful the sunset is!
3 What a messy room it is!
4 How attractive she is!
5 What an old house it is!
6 What a great time we had!
7 How wonderful you look today!
8 How well he dances!
9 What big eyes she has!
10 How tasty these cookies are!

B

1 What a big house you have!
2 What a good friend you are!
3 How expensive the watch is!
4 What a beautiful mountain it is!
5 How cute these children are!
6 How lucky I am!
7 How well she speaks French!
8 How amazing the story is!
9 What a great job you did!
10 How difficult these math exercises are!

WRAP UP
pp.116~117

A

1 What a nice picture it is!
2 How busy the street is!
3 What a tall building it is!
4 How beautiful the swan is!
5 How beautifully she sings!
6 What lovely weather it is!
7 What brave boys they are!

(해설)

1 ▶ 뒤에 「a+형용사+명사」가 이어지므로 What이 알맞다.
2 ▶ 「How+형용사+주어+동사!」의 어순이 되어야 하므로 the
street is가 알맞다.
3 ▶ 「What+a+형용사+명사+주어+동사!」의 어순이 되어야
하므로 a tall building이 알맞다.
4 ▶ 「How+형용사+주어+동사!」의 어순이 되어야 하므로
beautiful이 the swan 앞에 와야 한다.
5 ▶ 뒤에 「부사+주어+동사!」가 이어지므로 How가 알맞다.
6 ▶ weather는 셀 수 없는 명사이므로 a를 빼야 한다.

7 ▸ 뒤에 「형용사＋명사＋주어＋동사」가 이어지므로 What이 알맞다. brave boys가 복수이므로 a는 쓰이지 않았다.

B

1 How shy he is!

2 What a great landscape it is!

3 What a nice hat you have!

4 How small these shirts are!

5 How fast she works!

C **1** ③ **2** ④

해설

1 ▸ 명사구(surprising news)를 강조하는 감탄문은 What으로 시작한다.

2 ▸ '비싼 차'는 an expensive car이고 「an＋형용사＋명사」 앞에는 What이 온다.

개념 Review

❶ 감정 ❷ 형용사

❸ 명사 ❹ 형용사/부사

UNIT **02** 명령문

PRACTICE **1** p.118

1 Answer **2** Be

3 Wash **4** Walk

해설

긍정 명령문은 '～해라'의 의미로 동사원형으로 시작한다.

PRACTICE **2** p.119

1 Don't play **2** Don't forget

3 Don't be **4** Don't eat

해설

부정 명령문은 '～하지 마라'의 의미로 「Don't＋동사원형」 형태이다.

문법 쏙쏙 pp.120~121

A

1 Open **2** Hurry

3 be **4** Stop

5 Turn down **6** move

7 Put on **8** wash

9 fight **10** help

11 Have **12** yell

해설

1, 2, 4, 5, 6, 7, 8, 10, 11 ▸ 긍정 명령문은 '～해라'의 의미로 동사원형으로 시작한다. 명령문 앞이나 뒤에 please를 붙이면 보다 공손한 표현이 된다.

3, 9, 12 ▸ 부정 명령문은 '～하지 마라'의 의미로 「Don't＋동사원형」 형태이다.

B

1 Wash **2** Don't touch

3 Be **4** Drink

5 Don't make **6** Help

7 Have **8** wait

9 Don't stand **10** Open

11 Come **12** Set

13 Be **14** Don't forget

15 don't go

해설

1, 3, 4, 6, 7, 8, 10, 11, 12, 13 ▸ 긍정 명령문은 '～해라'의 의미로 동사원형으로 시작한다. 명령문 앞이나 뒤에 please를 붙이면 보다 공손한 표현이 된다.

2, 5, 9, 14, 15 ▸ 부정 명령문은 '～하지 마라'의 의미로 「Don't＋동사원형」 형태이다. 명령문 앞이나 뒤에 please를 붙이면 보다 공손한 표현이 된다.

영작 술술 pp.122~123

A

1 Clean your room.

2 Help me with my homework.

3 Don't play the piano at night.

4 Listen carefully and answer the question.

5 Don't touch my things.

6 Please sit on the chair.

7 Don't drink too much coffee.

8 Be careful when you drive a car.

9 Don't take photos in the museum.

10 Don't be late again. Okay?

B

1 Save energy.

2 Don't press the button.

3 Wear your seatbelt, please.

   [Please wear your seatbelt.]

4 Put away your toys.

5 Don't worry about it.

6 Turn off your cell phone.

7 Don't follow his advice.

8 Take off your shoes indoors.

9 Don't shout in front of the library.

10 Don't make any noise.

WRAP UP

pp.124~125

A

1 Have some food.

2 Don't eat too many sweets.

3 Help yourself.

4 Don't make a mess.

5 Be careful.

6 Do your homework.

7 Don't leave the door open.

해설

1▸ 긍정 명령문은 동사원형으로 시작하므로 Do have → Have

2▸ 부정 명령문은 「Don't+동사원형」 형태이므로 Not eat → Don't eat

3▸ Help yourself(마음껏 드십시오)는 긍정 명령문이므로 동사원형인 Help로 시작해야 알맞다.

4▸ 부정 명령문은 「Don't+동사원형」 형태이므로 Don't making → Don't make

5▸ 형용사 careful은 '조심하는'이고, '조심하다'는 「be동사+careful」로 나타낸다. Do → Be

6▸ 긍정 명령문은 동사원형으로 시작하므로 Does → Do

7▸ 부정 명령문은 「Don't+동사원형」 형태이므로 Leave not → Don't leave

B

1 Sign here, please.[Please sign here.]

2 Go and have fun.

3 Wash your hands before dinner.

4 Don't drink too much soda.

5 Don't forget your umbrella.

C **1** ② **2** ③

해설

1▸ 부정 명령문은 「Don't+동사원형」 형태이므로 turning → turn

2▸ '두려워하다'는 be afraid이고, 부정 명령문이므로 Don't be가 와야 알맞다.

개념 Review

❶ 동사원형 ❷ please ❸ Don't

ACTUAL TEST

pp.126~127

01 ④	02 ④	03 ④	04 ①
05 ②			

06 What an interesting movie it is!

07 Don't jump on the bed.

08 ④	09 ④	10 ②	11 ③
12 ④	13 ③		

14 How exciting the game is!

15 Don't be late for school again.

01 명사구(beautiful day)를 강조하는 감탄문은 What으로 시작하고, day는 셀 수 있는 명사이므로 a까지 써야 알맞다.

02 '그 문을 만지지 마'라는 부정 명령문이므로 touch 앞에 don't가 와야 한다.

03 명사구(a nice car)를 강조하는 감탄문이므로 What으로 시작하고 「What+a+형용사+명사+주어+동사!」의 어순이다.

04 형용사(happy)를 강조하는 감탄문은 「How+형용사+주어+동사!」의 어순이다.

05 첫 번째 빈칸 뒤에는 명사구인 kind people이 이어지므로 What으로 시작하는 감탄문이 알맞고, 두 번째 문장은 '도서관에서는 조용히 해라'라는 의미의 긍정 명령문이므로 빈칸에 동사원형 Be가 와야 한다.

06 What으로 시작하는 감탄문은 「What(+a/an)+형용사+명사+주어+동사!」의 어순이다.

07 부정 명령문은 「Don't+동사원형」 형태이다.

08 ①, ②, ③은 뒤에 「형용사/부사+주어+동사!」가 이어지므로 How가 알맞고, ④는 뒤에 명사구인 「형용사+명사」 형태가 이어지므로 What이 알맞다.

09 감탄문에서 맨 마지막의 「주어+동사」는 생략할 수 있다.

10 「How+형용사+주어+동사!」의 어순이 되어야 하므로 How sweet you are!로 고쳐야 알맞다.

11 긍정 명령문은 동사원형으로 시작한다. Please는 보다 공손히 표현하기 위해 추가되었다. sits → sit

12 '큰 도시'는 a big city이며 명사구를 강조하는 감탄문은 「What(+a/an)+형용사+명사+주어+동사!」의 어순이다.

13 부정 명령문은 「Don't+동사원형」 형태이다.

14 How로 시작하는 감탄문은 「How+형용사/부사+주어+동사!」의 어순이다.

15 부정 명령문은 「Don't+동사원형」 형태이다.

WORKBOOK ANSWERS

UNIT **01** 감각동사 / 수여동사
pp.2~3

A

1 cold		**2** O
3 you		**4** O
5 O		**6** elegant
7 O		**8** me
9 strong		**10** beautiful
11 us		**12** O
13 O		**14** her niece
15 O			

B

1 The bread smells buttery.

2 Did you lend her some money?

3 The ice cream tastes sweet.

4 The rain sounds soft.

5 I sent my cousin a birthday invitation.

6 The rainbow looks colorful after the rain.

7 Grace gave her friend a colorful bracelet.

8 She showed me a photo of her cat.

9 The breeze feels gentle and cool.

10 Harry wrote his teacher an email.

UNIT **02** 목적보어를 갖는 동사
pp.4~5

A

1 neat		**2** her cat
3 Angela		**4** us
5 a success		**6** beautiful
7 her		**8** difficult
9 her		**10** her kitten
11 open		**12** him
13 interesting		**14** the mayor
15 happy			

B

1 The chef left the soup hot on the stove.

2 The scientist named his new discovery Solaris.

3 The computer makes the tasks efficient.

4 I found the manual very helpful.

5 The zookeeper named the baby elephant Peanut.

6 I found the math test difficult.

7 His creativity made him a great inventor.

8 We call our teacher Ms. Brown.

9 She left the window closed.

10 We elected Michael the captain of the team.

UNIT **01** Can / May
pp.6~7

A

1 can		**2** can't
3 may		**4** May I
5 can		**6** can't
7 may		**8** can't
9 may		**10** can
11 may not		**12** can't
13 may		**14** may not
15 May I			

B

1 My sister can speak French fluently.

2 You may park your car in the designated area.

3 I can help you with your homework.

4 We can have a picnic in the park.

5 I may go to Italy during winter vacation.

6 She may arrive late to the party.

7 We can't afford to buy a new car.

8 This old car may break down.

9 Can she bake delicious cakes?

10 May I have your assistance with this task?

A

1	must	**2**	must
3	must	**4**	must
5	must	**6**	have to
7	must	**8**	must
9	must	**10**	have to
11	mustn't	**12**	must
13	have to	**14**	don't have to
15	have to		

B

1 You must[have to] finish your homework by 5:00 p.m.

2 They must be going on a picnic.

3 You mustn't eat too much junk food.

4 We must[have to] be at the airport by 8:00 a.m.

5 Do they have to wear uniforms to school?

6 People mustn't smoke in this area.

7 We must[have to] leave early.

8 He must be preparing for an exam.

9 Students mustn't use their phones during class.

10 He doesn't have to wake up early tomorrow.

Chapter 03 비교

A

1 harder, hardest

2 lazier, laziest

3 younger, youngest

4 closer, closest

5 louder, loudest

6 dirtier, dirtiest

7 slower, slowest

8 nicer, nicest

9 slimmer, slimmest

10 braver, bravest

11 busier, busiest

12 warmer, warmest

13 fatter, fattest

14 more popular, most popular

15 more interesting, most interesting

B

1 taller than

2 the most popular

3 more expensive than

4 the heaviest

5 hotter than

6 the fastest

7 the newest

8 bigger than

9 the oldest

10 softer than

A

1	less	**2**	more
3	good	**4**	much
5	less	**6**	many
7	least	**8**	worse
9	more	**10**	best
11	louder, louder	**12**	least
13	much	**14**	better
15	fastest		

B

1 Helping others is a good thing.

2 The eagle is one of the fastest birds in the sky.

3 My sister has less homework than I do.

4 I have more apples than oranges in the basket.

5 The least exciting part of the movie was the beginning.

6 I received a worse grade than Ryan.

7 The water in the pot is getting hotter and hotter.

8 The ocean is much bigger than the lake.

9 Reading every day can make you a better reader.

10 The rocket is much faster than the airplane.

Chapter 04 전치사

UNIT 01 시간의 전치사
pp.14~15

A

1	at	**2**	after
3	on	**4**	during
5	on	**6**	until
7	in	**8**	before
9	from, to	**10**	in
11	for	**12**	at
13	in	**14**	in
15	until		

B

1 We often go hiking on the weekend.
2 We will be camping for three days.
3 The concert is held on a summer night in July.
4 I like to read books on rainy days.
5 Please wash your hands before dinner.
6 The store's grand opening is at 10:00 a.m.
7 The library is open from Monday to Saturday.
8 I love to swim on hot days.
9 I will be on vacation in Spain in August.
10 You can play outside until sunset.

UNIT 02 장소의 전치사
pp.16~17

A

1	on	**2**	under
3	in front of	**4**	in
5	across from	**6**	in
7	between	**8**	on
9	in front of	**10**	in
11	behind	**12**	next to
13	in	**14**	across from
15	between		

B

1 The children are swimming in the pool.
2 The children were playing behind the house.
3 The kids are playing soccer on the playground.
4 There is a statue in front of City Hall.
5 I found the toy under the sofa.
6 There is a small garden between the two houses.

7 He is fixing his car in the garage.
8 My dad placed the gift box in front of me.
9 The pen is next to the notebook.
10 There is a convenience store across from the hotel.

Chapter 05 접속사

UNIT 01 등위 접속사
pp.18~19

A

1	and	**2**	but	**3**	and
4	and	**5**	or	**6**	but
7	so	**8**	but	**9**	or
10	and	**11**	so	**12**	but
13	and	**14**	or	**15**	so

B

1 She is skilled and dedicated.
2 My laptop is powerful but heavy.
3 Ted is reading a book, and I am studying.
4 Are you interested in painting or sculpture?
5 The food was delicious, or I was hungry.
6 The movie was long but exciting.
7 She is talented at singing and dancing.
8 The coffee was bitter, so I put some sugar in it.
9 Do you want to have pizza or pasta?
10 He is tired, but he needs to finish his work.

UNIT 02 종속 접속사
pp.20~21

A

1 before I leave for school
2 After we bake cookies
3 Because I was thirsty
4 If it is sunny
5 after the concert was over
6 when the soil feels dry
7 before I go for a run
8 if you are patient
9 because it was expensive
10 when it is raining outside

B

1 When the sun sets, the sky turns orange and pink.

2 You will be late for school if you walk.

3 You have to do your homework before you watch TV.

4 Because the weather was hot, I turned on the fan.

5 After the play ended, the actors greeted the audience.

6 The stars twinkle when the night sky is clear.

7 I always wear a seatbelt because it keeps me safe.

8 If we exercise regularly, our bodies become strong.

9 After we turned off the lights, we left the classroom.

10 Before the party starts, we decorate the room.

Chapter 06 감탄문과 명령문

UNIT 01 감탄문

pp.22~23

A

1	What	2	How	3	What
4	What	5	How	6	What
7	How	8	What	9	What
10	How	11	What	12	How
13	How	14	What	15	How

B

1 What great athletes they are!

2 How slowly the snail moves!

3 What sad news it is!

4 What a tall building it is!

5 How exciting the game is!

6 What a comfortable sofa it is!

7 How beautiful the stars are!

8 How cozy this bed is!

9 What an incredible voice you have!

10 How happily they danced at the party!

UNIT 02 명령문

pp.24~25

A

1	Close	2	wear
3	Feed	4	Be honest
5	Call	6	read
7	check	8	Finish
9	run	10	waste
11	be noisy	12	open

B

1 Please speak louder.[Speak louder, please.]

2 Don't be sad. There is always hope.

3 Apologize when you make a mistake.

4 Don't park your car here, please.
   [Please don't park your car here.]

5 Look both ways before crossing the street.

6 Don't litter on the street.

7 Share your toys with your friends.

8 Don't bite your nails. It's a bad habit.

9 Please pay attention to the lecture.
   [Pay attention to the lecture, please.]

10 Don't throw away that paper, please.
   [Please don't throw away that paper.]